Library of
Davidson College

# The Greens of West Germany:
## Origins, Strategies, and Transatlantic Implications

Robert L. Pfaltzgraff, Jr.
Kim R. Holmes
Clay Clemens
Werner Kaltefleiter

**Special Report**
August 1983

INSTITUTE FOR FOREIGN POLICY ANALYSIS, INC.
Cambridge, Massachusetts, and Washington, D.C.

**Requests for copies** of IFPA Special Reports should be addressed to the Circulation Manager, Special Reports, Institute for Foreign Policy Analysis, Central Plaza Building, Tenth Floor, 675 Massachusetts Avenue, Cambridge, Massachusetts 02139 (Telephone: 617-492-2116). Please send a check or money order for the correct amount along with your order.

**Standing orders** for all Special Reports will be accepted by the Circulation Manager. Standing order subscribers will automatically receive all future Special Reports as soon as they are published. Each Report will be accompanied by an invoice.

IFPA also maintains a **mailing list** of individuals and institutions who are notified periodically of new Institute publications. Those desiring to be placed on this list should write to the Circulation Manager, Special Reports, at the above address.

A list of IFPA publications appears on the inside back cover.

The Institute for Foreign Policy Analysis, Inc., incorporated in the Commonwealth of Massachusetts, is a tax-exempt organization under Section 501(c)(3) of the U.S. Internal Revenue Code, and has been granted status as a publicly-supported, nonprivate organization under Section 509(a)(1). Contributions to the Institute are tax-deductible.

Copyright © 1983 by the Institute for Foreign Policy Analysis, Inc.
First Edition

Library of Congress Catalog Card No. 83-048704

ISBN 0-89549-056-0

Printed by Corporate Press, Inc., Washington, D.C.

# Contents

Preface — v

Summary Overview — vii

The Greens: Implications for the United States — 1
*by Robert L. Pfaltzgraff, Jr.*

The Origins, Development, and Composition of the Green Movement — 15
*by Kim R. Holmes*

  Historical Background: Themes, Forerunners and Legacies — 15

  Postwar Trends of Discontent in West Germany — 19

  From the Student Movement to the Rise of the Greens — 26

  The Social and Political Composition of the Green Movement — 39

The Green Program for German Society and International Affairs — 47
*by Clay Clemens*

  The Green View of German Society — 50

    Green Criticisms of Modern German Society — 50

    Evaluating the Criticisms — 53

    Green Alternatives for Germany — 56

    Evaluating the Alternatives — 60

  The Green View of International Affairs — 68

    Green Criticisms of the West's Foreign Policy — 68

    Evaluating the Criticisms — 72

    Green Alternatives for the West — 76

    Evaluating the Alternatives — 80

  Conclusion — 83

The Greens/Alternatives and the Peace Movement:
A Challenge to the German Party System 86
*by Werner Kaltefleiter*

The Greens/Alternatives:
A Uniquely German Movement? 86

The Structure of the Greens/Alternatives 87

The Greens/Alternatives as an Ecological Group:
The First Phase 90

The Greens/Alternatives as a Left-Wing Fundamental Opposition
Party: The Second Phase 93

The Future of the Greens/Alternatives 100

Implications for German Politics 102

Conclusion 105

# Preface

On December 12, 1979, the North Atlantic Council took the unanimous decision to modernize NATO nuclear capabilities, following a period of protracted discussions within the governments of NATO members and within the Alliance itself. The decision provided for the deployment of 108 Pershing II ballistic missiles in the Federal Republic of Germany to replace an equivalent number of aging shorter-range Pershing I systems, and the stationing of a total of 464 ground launched cruise missiles in Belgium, Britain, the Federal Republic, the Netherlands and Italy. It is instructive to recall that the NATO decision was prompted initially by West European apprehensions that the Soviet Union, by its deployment of the SS-20 since the end of 1976, was tilting the balance of Eurostrategic forces ominously in its favor, while the SALT II Treaty, then under negotiation, did nothing to constrain Soviet SS-20 deployment.

In the years since the 1979 NATO decision Western Europe and the Atlantic Alliance have confronted a series of protest movements, whose focus initially was the Federal Republic of Germany, but which spread to the Netherlands, Belgium and Britain. The rise of opposition in West Germany attracted special attention because of the pivotal position of the NATO Central Front for the forward defense of Western Europe. The Federal Republic furnishes the territory and manpower that are indispensable to the Alliance. The deployment of newer generation NATO nuclear systems was envisaged as a means of reinforcing the deterrence links of the Alliance, for the Soviet Union could not invade Western Europe without the presumption that NATO nuclear forces and strategic systems deployed in the United States itself would be launched against the Soviet Union. In short, although they have ranges substantially less than that of the SS-20, the Pershing II and ground launched cruise missiles have sufficient capability to ensure that some military targets in the Soviet Union could be attacked if Moscow chose to launch an act of aggression against NATO. Thus, the deployment of such systems by the United States, with the official support of other NATO members, was designed to furnish tangible evidence of the American resolve to take whatever risks might be necessary to fulfill its security commitment to the Atlantic Alliance.

If new generation NATO nuclear systems could not be deployed in the Federal Republic of Germany, the most vitally important sector of the forward defense of NATO would have been effectively decoupled from the nuclear umbrella of the Alliance. However, the rise of opposition in the Federal Republic had other unsettling implications. A substantial portion of the opposition to NATO within West Germany held membership in the Green movement, which has attracted attention because it embodies certain characteristics drawn from the German past—for example, early nineteenth century anti-industrial romanticism together with a sense of alienation from many of the values of the free societies of the West. Nevertheless, the Greens also seem to be a West German manifestation of a counterculture that has also emerged in the United States and elsewhere and, therefore, is worthy of study for possible insights into the problems likely to face the United States and other industrially advanced societies as a result of movements having some of the principal characteristics of the Greens.

The purpose of this study is to trace the origins of the Green movement, to assess its impact upon the Federal Republic of Germany, and to examine its implications for the United States. This Special Report forms part of a series of studies to be published under the auspices of the Institute for Foreign Policy Analysis. These publications, based upon research and analysis by the Institute, are designed to assess, on a comparative basis, political-societal trends and movements in the United States and Western Europe, together with their implications, existing and potential, for the national security and domestic policies of the United States in the years ahead. The preparation of this Special Report was made possible by a grant to the Institute from the Anschutz Family Foundation.

Robert L. Pfaltzgraff, Jr.
President
Institute for Foreign Policy Analysis, Inc.

# Summary Overview

Within the past five years, a new force has emerged on the West German political scene, one with troubling implications for both Western security and the future of free societies. The Green movement, although numerically small, has come to exert a disproportionate influence over the discourse of public policy because it encompasses various streams of current anti-Establishment protest and countercultural ideas, along with an appeal to certain traditional symbols from Germany's past. Above all, the Greens have become the focus of both resistance to nuclear deterrence and support for neutralism. Given the Federal Republic's critical importance, the defense of Western values and institutions against erosion from within and pressure from the outside requires a clear understanding of the Greens, their origins, programs and future prospects.

## Implications for the United States

It is important that Americans understand the significance of the Greens, for the movement's transatlantic implications are evident. Whatever their characteristically German aspects, many Green themes have been heard in the United States before and retain a certain appeal on the American Left. The ideas espoused by the Greens have gained increasing support within the so-called "peace movement" in the United States since the beginning of the present decade. Strong transatlantic links have emerged between the Greens in the Federal Republic and counterpart groups in the United States. Moreover, the Green movement has generated a virulent anti-Americanism in certain circles in the Federal Republic. The themes espoused by the Greens, which for the most part closely resemble policy positions taken by the Soviet Union, serve the Soviet goal of weakening, dividing and confusing the West while Moscow's vast military buildup proceeds unaffected by any comparable opposition within the Soviet Union. It is not surprising that Moscow has attempted to exploit the advantages that have accrued from the emergence of the Greens—and other elements of the "peace movement"—by means of Soviet activities that include attempts to manipulate such groups and an intensive propaganda campaign in support of policies designed to prevent NATO from modernizing its military capabilities.

## The Greens' Evolution and Composition

Although the Greens are a recent phenomenon, they do not lack historical roots. Indeed, their movement is heir to certain traditions in the history of German social and political thought: a vague romanticism that rejects the complex realities of modern life, above all, technological progress; the related theme of cultural despair, with its contempt for "unaesthetic" industrial society and parliamentary institutions; the anarchist contempt for state authority; and the utopian socialist emphasis on collectivism instead of individualism. All of these traditions today, as in the past, strike a responsive chord among some young people and intellectuals who lack experience in dealing with everyday life and the complexities of public policy.

While the Greens consciously, or unconsciously, reflect these historical attitudes, they also manifest the more contemporary streams of opposition to West Germany's inclusion in the Western security system—such as the protest campaign of the 1950s—and the radically anticapitalist, antiparliamentary activism of the 1960s student movement. They hammer away at similar themes: fear of nuclear weapons and contempt for party politics and bureaucratic administration.

In the Greens, these past and relatively recent traditions came to be blended with the much more contemporary message of environmentalism. The 1970s revived in Germany and elsewhere an emotional critique of industrial growth and its effects, along with simplistic formulas for the return to a less complex, natural life-style. These disparate groups throughout the decade mobilized sentiment first against local and then against regional projects, especially nuclear power plant construction.

Given such a mixed background, it is not surprising that the Greens have evolved as a heterogeneous movement, which has included an ecological campaign that is anticapitalist in tone and eventually harmonized with the leftism of ex-student radicals. Rejecting all established political parties, the Green movement's component groups soon came together as a loosely united front. They campaigned in local and regional elections, meeting with immediate success in certain areas. Eventually they developed a national organization and participated in the Federal German elections of 1980 and 1983. The nationwide issue that cemented the movement together was protest against NATO nuclear force modernization, and the Greens became a central element and organizational center of the "peace movement" in Germany.

Nonetheless, the movement's composition has remained heterogeneous, and today there are varying degrees of emphasis on issues and differing levels of leftist influence across its constituent groups—from the "back-to-nature" Greens of Baden-Württemberg to the left-wing nationalist "Alternatives" of Berlin. Each group has a different answer to the question of how best to deal with political rivals in the regional parliaments. At the same time the movement's social composition in all areas is dominated by youths and intellectuals, those most disenchanted with modern society and most prone to idealistic or radical alternatives.

## Green Views on Policy

In light of this evolution, it is not surprising that the Greens have no common, coherent program. Instead, their statements on policy are often contradictory, hypercritical of current policy, and hopelessly utopian when it comes to alternatives to existing political structures, economic systems, and national security policies. They claim to see enormous domestic ills in current German society, attributable to the "growth imperative," consumerism, and the technological impulse, as well as to allegedly oligarchical control over all institutions. These charges often border on paranoia and scare-mongering, and display an elitist scorn for a prosperity the Greens already enjoy but would deny to others. Most of the accusations against current policy are disingenuous, inaccurate or unjustified.

As for their vision of Germany's domestic future, the Greens demand sweeping, fundamental change—an economy based on conservation, "soft energy" sources, consumer testing, wage equalization, shorter work time, mass transit, decentralized administration, all based on the premise that productivity will take care of itself if living conditions are ecologically acceptable. Economic decisions would be entirely subordinated to "social" goals as well—equal rights and minority rights—while political life would be dominated by "extra-parliamentary" methods. All of these socio-economic changes are vague, resting on untested or impractical concepts, plagued by contradictions between ecological goals and job creation; productivity is taken for granted, costs and management overlooked. Doubts about the feasibility of "grass roots" political control and "plebiscite" government, both of which favor activists and are of questionable democratic virtue, are dismissed.

In foreign affairs, the Greens consider all conflict the result of a superpower struggle that has nothing to do with conflicting values and institutions. The Soviets are seen as merely one partner in the dangerous game, no more threatening than the United States, which has been allegedly guilty of "accelerating the arms race." Germany is depicted as a victim because it lies at the heart of the superpower contest: it will be the "nuclear battlefield" in any future war in Europe. NATO nuclear modernization is pictured as a major contributing factor to the potential for conflict, despite the fact that the Soviet Union, not the United States, possesses the largest military capabilities in Europe. The Third World, too, is viewed as another exploited pawn of the superpowers, but especially of the United States.

The Greens' critique ignores the dynamics of East-West conflict, including the Soviet need for expansion to compensate for domestic failures. The Greens refuse to see the advantage that the Kremlin gains from flaunting its might. To bolster their claims of a "no fault" conflict between East and West, they draw absurd parallels between East and West, indulge in extreme anti-Americanism, display sympathy for the Soviet Union, and attempt to stir up a sense of national victimization among their fellow Germans.

In advancing alternative plans for Western policy, the Greens claim that a West Germany under their influence will shed all nuclear weapons and form a "nuclear-free zone" with communist East Germany that would begin the overall process of total disarmament in Europe. The superpowers, it is said, would be unable to resist this "wave of peace," as "public opinion" would dictate that disarmament continue. In place of any future weapons, Germans would rely on "social defense"—strikes and general uncooperativeness that would supposedly discourage aggression. This entire scheme naively assumes that tactics and appeals to peace which sway Western opinion will function in societies totally controlled by dictatorial regimes; communist systems are depicted as subject to the whims of public opinion. Even worse, the Greens suggest complete rhetorical neutralism so as not to annoy Moscow and slow this process. "Social defense" is backed by the absurd claim that countries can never be occupied against the will of their populations—this from a country bordering the entire Soviet bloc. The Greens' program is an elaborate scheme of self-neutralization that would willingly give up the West's free institutions to avoid the perceived risks of armed conflict.

### The Greens' Political Status and Prospects

How does a party with this type of program fit into the Federal Republic's political culture? The hard core includes communists and religious pacifists as well as ecologists—"the true believers"—and these groups all try to exercise control over Green movement policy. Given the Green bias against central control and professional politics, the result is organizational chaos. An outer circle of potential demonstrators forms the "rank and file," while a broader group—8 to 10 percent of the electorate—is willing to vote for the Greens. Finally, a large minority, perhaps 40 percent of all Germans, welcomes the Greens as a protest against the "Establishment," but does not support the movement.

Initially, the Green electorate consisted of people who voted for the movement as a means of expressing discontent with some local government policy—a nuclear power plant project, for example. Eventually the

Greens shifted their emphasis from regional to national issues like disarmament, and the movement's support became broader and more evenly distributed. They became the focus of anti-Establishment, primarily left-wing, protest, and thus began to drain votes from the Social Democrats (SPD). Under Helmut Schmidt, the SPD had shifted toward the political center, gradually abandoning its traditional position as the "party of change" and the left-wing themes of Willy Brandt. By becoming the "Establishment" under Schmidt, it lost more radical supporters to the Greens. Polls show that while Green voters distance themselves from all other parties, they are closer to the SPD than any of the others.

Thus, the question of the Greens' future is inseparable from that of the SPD's own course. Already under its new leadership, the SPD has shifted back to the left to co-opt Green issues and regain lost supporters; as a result, the Greens' vote total in the March 1983 election was lower than many expected, although they received sufficient electoral support to gain representation in the West German Bundestag. While the SPD can be expected to continue along this path of "reintegrating" the Greens, it faces the prospect of simultaneously alienating centrist voters. It will take at least several years for the party to strike the appropriate balance between left and center, which may virtually assure the present CDU/CSU-FDP government at least another term in office—assuming it makes no unforeseeable, major blunders.

The political significance of the Greens, then, lies in the potential that some of the issues that they espouse will be integrated into the political platforms of other groups, including the SPD in the Federal Republic; that they will be manipulated and exploited by the Soviet Union to disrupt NATO modernization; and that links between the Greens and counterpart organizations in the United States will continue to be strengthened as an attempt is made among such groups to solidify a transatlantic network detrimental to the purposes of the Atlantic Alliance, and to the domestic policies and national security interests of the United States and its allies.

# The Greens: Implications for the United States

## by Robert L. Pfaltzgraff, Jr.

Many of the themes that constitute the political ideology of the Greens are familiar to even the casual observer of American society. Their activism is directed against the political and economic foundations of a contemporary political system—the Federal Republic of Germany—that, as in the United States, has given unprecedented political freedom, social mobility, and economic advantage to its population. Like their counterparts elsewhere, the Greens seem to be largely without memory even of the recent past—a large percentage of members were born in the second half of this century—for the Federal Republic of Germany represents an achievement beyond the imagination and comprehension of any German (or anyone else) who gazed at the carnage and devastation, the poverty and psychological desolation, that existed at the end of World War II, from which at the time it appeared that Germany could not soon, if ever, recover.

This is not the place for an extended discussion either of the contribution of the United States, in the Marshall Plan, to the postwar rebirth of Europe, or for an assessment of the other reasons, including the capacity manifested by European peoples themselves to overcome Hitler's bitter legacy, that led to the remarkable post-World War II resurgence of Western Europe. Suffice it to assert here that the establishment of representative government, together with a dynamic private sector economy, provided the basis for the impressive achievements of the Federal Republic of Germany. Without the prosperity and political stability of the Federal Republic, the remainder of Western Europe—the states which became the core of an economically unifying Europe in the Common Market—could hardly have experienced the unprecedented growth rates that ushered in the age of mass consumption and economic abundance with living standards that historically had been reserved for the privileged few in Europe. In turn, even in the present decade, in which Western Europe has experienced economic reverses with rising unemployment and declining growth rates, the achievements of the Federal Republic and its neighbors to the West stand in stark contrast to the political and economic failures of communist states to the east, of which Poland is a constant reminder.

None of the successes registered in Western Europe would have been possible without the security guarantee furnished by the United States in the Atlantic Alliance. Here, it should be recalled that in the immediate aftermath of World War II the United States had demobilized the huge armies that had contributed decisively to the Allied victory. In contrast, the Soviet Union retained massive military capabilities that, together with the large communist parties of France and Italy, represented for the ravaged states of Western Europe an ominous threat in the years following World War II as the Soviet political grip tightened in Eastern Europe. It was the United States which provided economic and military assistance to European friends and allies, and ultimately the nuclear guarantee implicit in NATO, all of which contributed decisively to the rebuilding of Western Europe within a political framework of representative government. Undoubtedly, future historians will scrutinize the decades following World War II in order to discern the factors that led to Western Europe's transformation from destruction to prosperity, from despair to hope, from the wars that had gripped Europe in the first half of this century to a period of sustained peace, despite the expansionist policies of the Soviet Union. The generation that separated the two World Wars had been marked by the rise of communism and fascism in Europe, the growth of state control over political and economic life, economies in stagnation and depression, the imposition of barriers to international trade, and ultimately the outbreak of World War II.

It is instructive briefly to restate the factors that contributed to the reconstruction of Europe and to the security environment of the decades since World War II, because they have been the object of attack by the Greens in the Federal Republic and by assorted groups that, taken together, comprise an antidefense coalition whose critique extends in some cases to the present structure of the economies of the Federal Republic of Germany and the United States. A return to an agrarian society in place of modern industrialization, the replacement of large corporations and mass production with smaller economic units, and substitution of "self-realization" for the work ethic—themes which co-exist in the Green movement—are easily recognizable in many of the groups that, since the 1960s, have sprung up in the United States as part of a counterculture. The quest for an alternate life-style that supposedly brings narcissistic fulfillment for certain elements of society in a communal existence based upon the values of instant self-gratification that masquerades as individualism is found both in Western Europe and the United States. According to the Greens, income is to be independent of work, although even a superficial understanding of economics leads inevitably to the conclusion that the basis for wealth in a society lies ultimately in the productivity of its people and productivity has been directly proportional to the level of technology. Primitive societies are not noted for productivity or for wealth shared by large numbers of people. Although they scorn the technologically advanced societies of Western Europe and the United States, the Greens and their counterparts hold that modern science has opened the way to a new post-industrial civilization in which the role of work is diminished and the leisure orientation of society enhanced. They seek simultaneously to weaken the basis for the technological innovation necessary to sustain productivity in advanced societies and to benefit from the fruits of science that has enabled millions of people to enjoy higher living standards.

The muddled thought that comprises the Green economic program is apparent. No one can deny the importance of relieving mankind, to the extent possible, of disagreeable and menial labor, while providing a more abundant life in which leisure is enhanced. This is precisely what the private sector economies of the most advanced industrial states have achieved in Western Europe and in the United States to a degree without precedent. It should be contrasted with the experience of communist states, where independent workers associations, including trade unions, are banned and occupational choice is dictated and circumscribed by the needs of the state. The affluence of the working populations of the West, in contradistinction to their counterparts to the East, stands as a cruel reminder of the inherent inability of communist systems to achieve their principal self-proclaimed goal: the liberation of the proletariat. Instead, it is the Soviet Union, as Alexander Solzhenitsyn so eloquently states, which has oppressed workers in the name of communism and, when deemed necessary by the ruling Soviet elite, annihilated its opponents or placed them in mental hospitals or labor camps. As the Polish experience with the banned Solidarity union reminds us, the workers form members of an oppressed class in communist societies.

It is the Soviet Union, again in sharp contrast with the societies of the West, that has elevated to official dogma the tenets of an oppressive materialism in which the well-being of the individual is sacrificed on the altar of state interest. The forced collectivization of agriculture in communist states, with repeated failures of crops from mismanagement and misallocation of resources, the impressment of workers in the construction of the industrial infrastructure, and the monopolization of economic power by the state stand as brutal monuments to the Soviet concept of materialism. Collectivization and industrialization according to the needs of the state, as determined by a ruling elite not subject to popular election, separates the Soviet Union from the limited, constitutional, elected governments of the West.

In the final analysis, it is the diversity of, and the guarantee of freedom in, societies on both sides of the Atlantic, contrasted with the political regimentation of the Soviet Union, that paradoxically enable groups such as the Greens to exist, for opposition has no place in the Soviet political schema, as we are reminded whenever individuals or groups in the Soviet Union question the decisions of the ruling elite. The pluralism and representative political institutions of the Federal Republic have made possible the achievement of political recognition and status for movements such as the Greens, just as the freedom of our society has furnished the indispensable basis for a counterculture in the United States. While they decry the impact of advanced technologies upon society, such groups are often the direct beneficiaries of the technological age and, in particular, the electronic media. No such opportunities are available in totalitarian states such as the Soviet Union in which such groups are banned and in which, in any event, the media are tightly controlled by the political elite. Thus it must be inferred that the ideas represented by the Greens and analogous groups elsewhere exist under circumstances that are peculiar to industrialized, politically pluralistic societies that have placed themselves in the forefront of advanced technology and the granting of freedom to the individual.

The Greens represent a coalition that embraces environmentalists and the opponents of a strong defense. Because they do not approve of the society in which they live, they oppose the allocation of the resources necessary to provide for its security. Nuclear power, which they mistakenly hold despoils the environment, is as objectionable as nuclear weapons, which they condemn for their alleged implications for the inevitability of armed conflict. This is not the place for an extended critique of such misconceptions. Nuclear power plants have proved to be far safer than coal mining both for workers and for the surrounding environment. Nuclear weapons have never been used against other states which also possess such weapons; furthermore, states having nuclear weapons have not employed conventional capabilities against each other—a factor that may help to explain the peaceful era that Europe has enjoyed since the end of World War II. The possession of military capabilities by the United States and its allies has no purpose other than to defend pluralistic, free societies from the threats posed by an expansionist totalitarian power. Unlike Soviet/Warsaw Pact forces, NATO has no military strategy or force posture for the conduct of offensive military operations to the east. NATO is based upon a strategy that provides for a flexible *response* to an attack.

It is essential to place the Greens in proper perspective. In the Federal Republic of Germany, they presently constitute approximately 5 percent of the electorate, as measured in the support that they attracted in the election of March 6, 1983, although certain of their ideas formed part of the electoral campaign of the Social Democratic Party, which had governed the Federal Republic between 1969 and 1982 but was decisively defeated in March 1983. Although the vast majority of the West German electorate has rejected both the critique and the proposed remedies of the Greens, it would be imprudent to conclude that the threat posed by the Greens is insignificant because their numbers are not great as a percentage of the total electorate. History is strewn with examples of groups whose impact has been far greater than their numerical strength. Technologically advanced, politically pluralistic societies are particularly vulnerable to such groups, especially if their disruptive tactics extend to mass demonstrations designed to prevent the construction, for example, of nuclear power plants or the installation of modernized NATO nuclear systems, and if their tactics include resort to violence against opponents.

It is tempting to draw parallels between the Greens and the forces that brought the Weimar Republic to its knees. The announcement of the Greens after the election of March 6, 1983, that they would resort to necessary extra-parliamentary means to prevent the installation of modern NATO missiles brought to mind statements by the Nazis before the fall of the Weimar Republic. However, the Greens have no charismatic leader comparable to Adolph Hitler, nor do they possess the storm troops upon whom the Nazis regularly called to enforce their will in the streets and to disrupt the practice of representative government. Nevertheless, the lesson of that unfortunate era in German history is apparent: The survival of representative institutions depends upon the procedural consensus that sustains them—the commitment of the elected and the governed alike to certain principles of conduct based upon agreement about the acceptability of the political system. In the United States, unlike the Weimar Republic, our historic Constitutional debates have focused not upon the legitimacy of our political institutions, but instead have revolved about the interpretation of the Constitution, which symbolizes a commonly accepted and revered structure for the organization of our political affairs. The Weimar Republic, which preceded the rise of Hitler, was opposed by a broad spectrum of political groups—from monarchists to communists. If they could agree upon nothing else, together they held that the political structure embodied in the Weimar Republic was unacceptable as a framework for the realization of their, and Germany's, political goals.

In sharp contrast, the Federal Republic of Germany has enjoyed broadly based public support and, by the end of the present decade, will have had a longevity twice that of the Weimar Republic. But the Greens symbolize at least a fraying and perhaps a partial unraveling of the nearly universal support previously manifested for the present political and economic system in the Federal Republic of Germany. The more deeply rooted the representative political institutions and practices of a state, the greater its capacity to withstand forces that threaten procedural consensus or the constitutionalism that is the life blood of representative government. The emergence of groups committed to extra-legal activities based upon a rejection of the existing political structure is both a manifestation of the weakening of such institutions and a factor further contributing potentially to their deterioration. It is precisely because the roots of representative government in the Federal Republic do not have the depth of those of other states of the West that the Greens stir concern outside Germany. Here the principal question is whether the Greens signal the beginning of a progressive deterioration in the consensual basis that has sustained the Federal Republic.

Alternatively, does the movement represented by the Greens symbolize merely the German manifestation of a phenomenon that has its counterpart in other politically pluralistic, industrially advanced societies, including notably the United States, all of which supposedly will find it possible to cope successfully with the challenges posed by such groups? The fact remains that groups such as the Greens have already had a considerable impact upon political systems on both sides of the Atlantic, where governments have found it necessary to accommodate to demands for a greater emphasis upon arms control, without having had discernible comparable influence upon the armaments policies of the Soviet Union. The effect of the Greens and kindred groups is simultaneously to make more difficult the preservation of adequate levels of defense and to diminish any prospect for symmetrical arms reductions with the Soviet Union. Instead, the United States and its allies are pressed toward a unilateralism that would leave the Soviet Union in a militarily preponderant position.

Historically, the New World was shaped by peoples, political concepts, and economic ideas transplanted from Europe. Of equal importance has been the impact of the United States upon Europe from our colonial period to the late twentieth century. Since the end of World War II, the pace of interpenetration between America and Europe has quickened. Political fads and ideas generated in Europe are quickly transplanted across the Atlantic, and there is similar traffic in the opposite direction. The American bluejean youth culture of the 1960s attracted millions of adherents in many parts of the world, but nowhere more than in Europe where, as here, a kind of reverse chic sophistication came to be in vogue. The participants in antidefense rallies and ecology protest meetings in Bonn are indistinguishable, except in language, from those who have demonstrated in Washington, D.C. Both in style and substance, the counterculture of Berkeley, California, at the height of the Vietnam War has great similarity to some of the groups that have opposed the defense programs of the United States and its NATO allies in the early 1980s. The demonstrators on the streets of Amsterdam and London do not differ greatly in appearance, and in outlook, from those in New York and San Francisco. Similar causes—political, social, and economic—attract supporters from Los Angeles to Hamburg.

On both sides of the Atlantic, opponents of the armaments needed for the defense of free societies today from the threats posed by the Soviet Union follow in the footsteps of the anti-Vietnam coalition of the late 1960s. Without here entering into an extended discussion of the Vietnam War, it must be asserted, nevertheless, that the faulty assumptions upon which the Vietnam opponents based their argumentation have their counterpart in the case set forth today against defense policy by the Greens and by analogous groups in the United States. Central to this thesis is the flawed proposition that the United States bears a principal burden of responsibility for the international conflicts of the day and that unilateral steps on our part will contribute to a peaceful resolution on satisfactory terms. This theme constitutes a central element of Soviet propaganda and other Active Measures practiced by Moscow in a systematic effort to distort truth and to substitute myth for reality. Here, it is necessary to recall that the American withdrawal from Vietnam was followed, not by a mutually acceptable resolution of differences, but by the brutal use of force against our former allies and friends and the emergence of an oppressive state closely aligned with the Soviet Union bent upon the extension of hegemony over its Indochinese neighbors. The result has been the exodus of countless numbers of boat people from Vietnam—a pattern likely to be repeated in Central America if communist regimes continue to gain power there. In Germany, the wall that divides the Federal Republic from East Germany stands as an equally compelling reminder of the repression practiced by a communist regime against its own people—a large number of whom, when given the opportunity, have left in search of freedom in the West.

A preoccupation with the armaments policies of the United States, more than those of the Soviet Union, represents a theme of the so-called peace movement in Europe, including the Greens. Of course, there are no American nuclear missiles targeted against Western Europe. Only the Soviet Union deploys such capabilities which, in the case of the SS-20, increase by one new system each week. In fact, the stridency of the anti-*American* rhetoric of much of the so-called European peace movement has seemed to grow in direct proportion to the increase in the number of *Soviet* missiles aimed against Western Europe. Because it is impossible to convince the Soviet Union to remove such systems, the frustration of antidefense activists, both in Western Europe and the United States, can more easily be vented against the politically and morally sensitive governments of the West than against the obdurate monolithic Soviet state. Conceivably, those who oppose the deployment of NATO nuclear systems, such as the Pershing II and cruise missiles, fear that the stationing of such weapons in Europe will lead the Soviet Union to take whatever measures might be necessary either to forestall or to counter their deployment. Therefore, the United States and its European allies are urged not to deploy such systems in the hope that an appeased Soviet Union will eventually dismantle its SS-20s, or in the expectation at least that Moscow so placated will not be moved to heighten tensions and to destroy what remains of the tenuous legacy of detente.

Although there are presently no equivalent nuclear systems targeted from Western Europe against the Soviet Union (the SS-20 has a range four times that of the Pershing II and carries three warheads rather than the one warhead deployed on the Pershing II), the Soviet Union is rationalized to have built such capabilities for strictly "defensive" reasons, whatever that may mean, notwithstanding the fact that NATO has no plans to attack the Soviet Union and certainly does not possess either the military strategy or the military means that would be essential to any such goal. There exists no evidence in support of the proposition, and much to justify the contrary view, that an act of self-abnegation on the part of the United States in defense preparedness breeds any tendency toward emulation by the Soviet Union. The more the United States and its allies are moved toward unilateral arms reduction, the greater seems to be the Soviet incentive to achieve a politically decisive level of military superiority. In a telling statement, Petra Kelly, a leading figure of the Greens, has likened the Soviet SS-20 deployment to a cross to be borne by the peoples of the West, against which no countervailing capabilities must be deployed. All Soviet activity can be explained away in such terms if the fear exists that any Western response will produce, in turn, the potential for incautious behavior on the part of Moscow. Under such circumstances, of course, the ultimate result would be the monopolization of power in the hands of totalitarian states and possible martyrdom for those peoples who might finally choose in a desperate move to oppose such forces.

It is not necessary, however, to conjure up a "worst case scenario"—whether an attack by miscalculation launched by a confident Soviet Union against a unilaterally disarmed West, or an armed conflict undertaken by Western states, despite their military inferiority, in a last-ditch effort to preserve remaining vestiges of their independence as the "correlation of forces" shifted decisively in favor of the Soviet Union. The realization of the goals of the Greens would detach the Federal Republic of Germany politically, militarily, economically and psychologically from the West. Without the Federal Republic, NATO would be effectively dismantled, for there is no possibility of a forward defense without West German territory and manpower. It is for this reason that the Soviet Union has sought consistently to separate the Federal Republic from NATO and from its close political relationship with the United States. Thus, a neutralized Federal Republic of Germany, in keeping also with the ideas of the Greens, would represent the realization of one of the long-term goals of the Soviet Union. Further, a denuclearized Federal Republic, a goal of both the Greens and the Soviet Union, would be effectively decoupled from any American nuclear guarantee. All of the proposals put forward by the Soviet Union in the INF talks, providing for no NATO deployments while retaining for Moscow a monopoly in such land-based systems, would have the effect of separating the Federal Republic from the nuclear deterrence framework provided by the Atlantic Alliance. To make Germany a nuclear-free zone as advocated by members of so-called peace movements has no meaning unless it includes the territory—i.e., the Soviet Union—from which nuclear weapons can be launched against the territory of the supposedly nuclear-free zone. Both in the Federal Republic of Germany and in the United States we witness a tendency by self-proclaimed peace groups to declare nuclear-free zones. However compelling may be such a symbolic gesture to its proponents in the Greens and their counterparts elsewhere, they take no account of the fact that the nuclear-free zone itself is targeted by Soviet weapons. No such act of self-denial by those in the target areas is sufficiently strong to dismantle Soviet weapons systems.

Each of these themes forms part of a concerted Soviet campaign, whose purpose is to create a mental frame of reference, both in Western Europe and the United States, that applies one standard of conduct to the United States and another to the Soviet Union. Like much of the so-called peace movement, the Soviet Union would have us believe that the United States threatens the peace by building armaments vital to its security, notwithstanding the fact that the Soviet Union has now deployed the world's largest military capability. In responding with prudent defense programs, the United States is alleged to endanger peace. Although they have acknowledged their cooperation with the German Communist Party, which is aligned with Moscow, even the Greens reputedly balked at the blatant attempt made by the Soviet Union to dominate and manipulate discussions to plan demonstrations before President Reagan's visit to Bonn in June 1982. According to Ulrich Tost, a member of the Federal Council of the Greens: "The communists dominated the meeting completely. It took place under seemingly democratic rules, but that was a joke. We could barely get a word in."[1] The same meeting rejected a resolution that would have limited the "peace movement" to the use of nonviolent methods, voted decisively against a condemnation of Soviet intervention in Afghanistan, and opposed a motion calling for the lifting of martial law in Poland. In contrast, by a large majority, the meeting adopted a motion that condemned American policy in Central America and Southern Africa. All of these resolutions, of course, accord fully with Soviet policy.

Although it would be inaccurate to identify the Greens directly with the Soviet Union, it is equally shortsighted to fail to understand the importance attached by Moscow to the manipulation of such groups to promote the disarmament of the West. Since its founding in 1950 the Soviet front organization, the World Peace Council, formed to disseminate "Ban the Bomb" propaganda before the Soviet Union had acquired nuclear weapons, together with affiliated organizations in a large number of other countries, has conducted a worldwide campaign by means of conferences and publications in many languages, funded from Moscow, in support of Soviet interests, from the American withdrawal from Vietnam to the dismantling of U.S. defense capabilities in the present decade. At no time has the World Peace Council deviated from support for Soviet policy. West European governments have found it necessary to expel members of the Soviet KGB for complicity in the organization of demonstrations. For example, in April 1981, Vadim Leonov, a Soviet intelligence official operating in the guise of a newspaper correspondent, was ousted from the Netherlands. Before his departure, he stated: "If Moscow decides that 50,000 demonstrators must take to the streets in the Netherlands, then they take to the streets. Do you know how you can get 50,000 demonstrators at a certain place within a week? A message through my channels is sufficient."[2] Brezhnev is said to have awarded a medal to the Soviet Ambassador to the Netherlands, Aleksandr Yosiponich Romonov, for his contribution to Dutch demonstrations against NATO modernization.[3]

---

[1]Quoted in John Vinocur, "Peace Group Says Communists Dominated Talks on Bonn Protest," *International Herald Tribune* (Paris), April 6, 1982.
[2]Quoted in John Barron, *KGB Today: The Hidden Hand* (New York: Reader's Digest Press, 1983), p. 276.
[3]*Ibid.*, p. 273.

Although the idea of a nuclear freeze, which has gained such prominence in the United States in the early 1980s, has earlier antecedents, Brezhnev, in an address to the Twenty-Sixth Soviet Communist Party Congress on February 23, 1981, called for an immediate cessation in the production of nuclear weapons, including the INF modernization authorized by the NATO Ministerial Council on December 12, 1979. Less than a month after the Brezhnev proposal, a conference to plan strategy for the American campaign for a nuclear freeze was convened in Washington, D.C. It brought together groups and individuals who had long been active in various efforts to halt or to forestall needed U.S. defense programs. This is not the place for an extended discussion of the tactics and activities of the American nuclear freeze campaign. Suffice it to suggest that, like the program of the antinuclear activists of the Federal Republic, including the Greens, the effect of the nuclear freeze advocated by their American counterparts would be to leave in place the Soviet SS-20s targeted against Western Europe, as well as the vast arsenal of other Soviet counterforce-capable rockets, aimed against targets in the United States. This is clearly one of the objectives of the Soviet Union both in negotiations with the United States and in the campaign being waged by Moscow to shape public attitudes and deprive Western governments of needed support for defense. It can be inferred that the Soviet apparatus for the conduct of Active Measures, or political warfare, is being utilized as fully as possible for this purpose. According to FBI testimony during hearings held in July 1982 by the House Permanent Select Committee on Intelligence that did not receive as extensive publicity as they deserved:

We have information that some recruited Soviet agents in the peace movement were given instructions by the Soviets on actions to take. But we're well aware that the peace movement in Europe did have a very native and genuine spawning. Yet the Soviets were able to capitalize on that and drive it much farther than . . . the Europeans expected. We also have reporting . . . which shows that the Soviets tried to do the same thing in New York when they knew there was going to be a very large "peace" demonstration up there. The Soviets came in and tried to acquire all of the information they could about who was who in the peace movement, what coalitions were getting together, who were the key players, in order that they could begin to pressure them in the direction the Soviets wanted to go.[4]

Thus, the Soviet Union has sought to turn the issue of "peace" to its own purposes in activities on both sides of the Atlantic in an effort to influence the defense decisions of NATO members.

There remains the question of the impact of the Greens and other such groups upon the policies of the Federal Republic of Germany and the

---

[4]Quoted in *ibid.*, p. 290.

United States. Differences between the structure of the political systems of the Federal Republic and the United States hold implications for the tactics of the Greens and the so-called peace and ecology groups that have sprung up in the United States. To a far greater extent than the Federal Republic of Germany, with its system of limited proportional representation described elsewhere in this study, the political system of the United States does not favor third parties. Although a large number of political action groups devoted to the same types of issues as the Greens have arisen in the United States since the late 1960s, they presently have no visible prospect for coalescing in a political party strong enough to gain representation in the Congress, as the Greens have done in the Bundestag. As in the Federal Republic, however, their potential lies in the capacity that they manifest for influencing existing parties and, specifically, for having their programs co-opted by one of the major political parties. Such a process appears to be unfolding within the Democratic Party, or at least with some of its current presidential candidates, with respect to the American nuclear freeze movement, which has attracted substantial support and whose program would effectively codify the present disparities favoring the Soviet Union in certain important categories of weapons—the counterforce capable SS-20s targeted against Western Europe and the SS-18 against the United States—as well as prevent our much-needed strategic force modernization program and the planned INF deployment in Europe.

The opposition Social Democratic Party in the Federal Republic of Germany seeks to broaden to the left its electoral appeal by co-opting from the Greens many of the principal elements of their ecology-antidefense platform, and by dividing the Green core groups and ultimately isolating the most extreme elements, as described elsewhere in this study. Such a strategy by a left-of-center party has the effect of further isolating it from the mainstream center of the political spectrum, as has occurred in the British Labour Party since it was ousted from office by the Conservative Party of Prime Minister Thatcher and then overwhelmingly defeated in the election of June 1983. Similarly, the huge electoral victory of the Nixon Administration in 1972 is held to have been partly the result of the leftward movement of the Democratic Party under George McGovern, who had embraced the anti-Vietnam political coalition of that period. Such trends may seem immediately comforting to the proponents of centrist or conservative government, for they would appear to hold out the prospect for schisms to the left of the political spectrum between moderate and more extremist elements, again in keeping with the pattern of the British Labour Party and the process that has been apparent during much of the period since 1968 in the American Democratic Party and more recently in the Social Democratic Party in the Federal Republic of Germany.

Nevertheless, the politics of elections differ from the politics of governing. Winning electoral coalitions are usually not sufficiently broadly based to provide the consensus for an effective, consistent and sustained foreign policy and defense capability, especially if the opposition, or elements of it, consists of activist proponents of a fundamentally different set of policy priorities. For at least a generation preceding the late 1970s, the Federal Republic enjoyed both a foreign and domestic policy that rested upon a high level of substantive—as well as procedural—consensus. Such broadly based support has been diminished, with the Greens having both reflected and contributed to its decline. It will be recalled that the post-World War II policies of the United States that led to both the Marshall Plan and the formation of NATO, together with the emergence of the United States as a global power, rested upon a level of bipartisan support that was shattered in the late 1960s with the discord that accompanied the Vietnam War. The Greens and their counterparts elsewhere weaken, and reflect the weakening of, the consensus needed in pluralistic societies to make possible the conduct of an effective and consistent national security policy.

The implications of the decline in such consensus are apparent in the Federal Republic of Germany and the United States. In Bonn there exists a government strongly committed to NATO nuclear modernization in accordance with the dual-track decision taken by the Alliance in December 1979 but which must contend with a highly polarized opposition that seems prepared to resort to extra-legal means to thwart the completion of the deployment. Similar problems can be expected to face the Kohl Government on other issues, notably nuclear power plant construction, depending upon the extent to which opposition groups such as the Greens can mobilize support.

In the United States the legacy of a shattered foreign policy consensus is apparent in the opposition, under the simplistic slogan "No More Vietnams," to efforts by the Reagan Administration to assist forces seeking to oppose Soviet-Cuban supported groups in Central America. In an extreme—and it is to be hoped unlikely—scenario, the ideas represented by the Greens and their counterparts in the United States would become the dominant political force, with the political platform of the present majority relegated to a position from which they could either acquiesce in such programs or themselves seek to emulate the tactics of such groups in opposing the will of the new majority. To be sure, a society such as that advocated by the Greens would soon prove to be both ungovernable domestically and destabilizing in the international security environment. Conceivably, the Greens would be moved to take repressive action against their opponents on a scale and including measures not employed against them when they were in opposition.

Perhaps more likely, however, is the prospect, on both sides of the Atlantic, that such groups will continue to attempt to erode support for the policies in domestic affairs and in national security espoused by governments, and that their efforts will be undertaken either as part of political action organizations or as co-opted elements of an opposition political party, or with elements of both approaches. In either case, the task of strengthening the domestic foundations upon which economic growth can be nurtured and sustained with rising levels of productivity, together with the defense of the United States and its allies and friends from the security threats posed by the Soviet Union, will be made more difficult.

# The Origins, Development, and Composition of the Green Movement

*by Kim R. Holmes*

### Historical Background: Themes, Forerunners and Legacies

The Greens are fond of claiming that they represent something entirely new in the history of modern Europe. They are neither Left nor Right, they insist, but merely "ahead" of everyone else.[1] Whether they are indeed the avant-garde of some irreversible march of history, only time will tell; but it is nonetheless clear that they are not, historically speaking, entirely new. The Greens have certainly developed new political styles and formulated a new complex of ideas, best represented by the manner in which they have politicized the concept of ecology. But to an historian, the broad themes which run through the Green movement are suspiciously familiar, for the Greens are, despite their statements to the contrary, carriers of historical traditions whose origins reach as far back as the end of the 18th century. Understanding what these traditions are will provide historical insight into the ideas and aims of a political movement that has intentionally been long on novelty but short on history.

The Greens are, first of all, heirs to certain ideas in the German tradition of political romanticism. German Romanticism began at the end of the 18th century as a purely aesthetic revolt against the rationalism of the French Enlightenment. But what began as a cultural revolution soon took on political connotations as it became the intellectual nexus to a nationalist revolt against Napoleon in the Wars of Liberation. Whether cultural or political, German Romanticism was intended to achieve the triumph of romantic feeling over the tenets of reason. It celebrated the uniqueness of the individual, whose emotional insight was valued more than the ability to master discursive thinking, and it promised freedom from constraint and the exaltation of passion as the ideals of a new type of personal sensitivity. Whereas nature had been the model of reason to the French

---

[1]Ernst Hoplitschek, "Partei, Avantgarde, Heimat—oder was? Die 'Alternative Liste für Demokratie und Umweltschutz' in West-Berlin," in Jörg R. Mettke, editor, *Die Grünen. Regierungspartner von morgen?* (Reinbek and Hamburg: Rowohlt and Der Spiegel, 1982), p.100.

*philosophes*, to the German Romantics it became the source of romantic imagination and a link to mysteriously hidden truths.

Politically, German Romanticism became a vehicle for the rejection of Western liberalism and the emerging capitalist system which underpinned it. Sounding very much like a Green, the romantic nationalist Adam Müller once described Western capitalism as "the most general manifestation of that antisocial spirit, that arrogant egotism, that immoral enthusiasm for false reasoning."[2] Turning their backs on the Enlightenment's veneration of Greece and Republican Rome, the German Romantics praised the Middle Ages as the ideal model for a distinctly German type of political order. It was thought that the organic community of feudal times was far superior to the unheroic, legalistic parliamentarianism of England and the rationalistic republican democracy of France.

The romantic tradition of antimodernism was carried over into revolutionary conservatism, a political philosophy of the immediate post-World War I era that will be particularly relevant to the forthcoming discussion of conservative ecologists in the Green movement. Conservative revolutionaries emerged out of the crisis following Germany's defeat in World War I. Above all, they were cultural critics who, according to Fritz Stern, "sought to destroy the despised present in order to recapture an idealized past in an imaginary future."[3] The most influential spokesmen for revolutionary conservatism in the Weimar Republic were the intellectuals Moeller van den Bruck and Eduard Stadtler. Champions of a new kind of conservatism, they renounced not only the values of liberal industrial civilization but the pragmatic conservatism of Bismarck as well. Their conservatism was revolutionary because it had nothing tangible to conserve. It assaulted the entire spirit of industrial society of which Wilhelmine materialist conservatism was a crucial part.

The rejection of liberalism, materialism and capitalism, which had begun with the Romantics during the Napoleonic Era, was extended by intellectuals such as Moeller van den Bruck to encompass a sweeping condemnation of the spiritual values of the entire West. They singled out liberalism in particular as the embodiment of everything they scorned in the grave new world of modernity. In their estimation, liberalism was not only the spiritual foundation of modern decadence, it was also the foremost political expression of the materialism and scientific rationalism which they believed was eating away at the soul of German culture. The conservative

---

[2]Quoted from Hans Kohn, *The Mind of Germany: The Education of a Nation* (New York: Charles Scribner's Sons, 1960), p. 64.

[3]Fritz Stern, *The Politics of Cultural Despair: A Study in the Rise of the Germanic Ideology* (Berkeley and Los Angeles: University of California Press, 1961), xvi.

revolutionaries were, in this respect, just as much enemies of the materialist bourgeoisie as they were of the socialist proletariat. They wanted, in fact, to create a "German" socialism based on a vague Hegelian synthesis of cultural nationalism and corporate socialism. To the chagrin of Moeller van den Bruck, many of his ideas became incorporated into Nazi ideology, but his reservations about Hitler in the early days of the Nazi movement do not alter the fact that his philosophy was part of the cultural climate which gave rise to the ideology of the Third Reich.

Spiritual forerunners not only to the conservative ecologists but to the entire Green movement were the German cultural pessimists. The most popular exponent of cultural pessimism in the Weimar Republic was Oswald Spengler, the author of the eminently popular *The Decline of the West*. Drawing on the influences of Friedrich Nietzsche and the cultural reactionary Julius Langbehn, Spengler postulated that civilization was akin to a living organism that passed from youth through maturity to old age and decline.[4] The critique of Western Civilization by Spengler and other cultural pessimists was predicated on the assumption that liberalism and capitalism had suffocated the soul of human culture because they had destroyed the organic sense of community that was culture's social root. They believed that nothing original or inspirational would ever come out of the West again, and that the capitalist "traders" in England and the democrats in France would eventually destroy the new world of which they themselves were the authors. Like many conservative revolutionaries, Spengler envisioned a synthesis of Prussian culture and socialism as the best line of defense against the spread of Western decline to Germany. He thought this could be achieved by forging a great political alliance between the German Right and the socialist parties to combat the parliamentary system—the "inner England"—of the Weimar Republic.[5] The rejection of the idea of progress, and the sense that materialist civilization had reached its end, are cultural assumptions that will re-emerge, in modified form, in the Greens' cultural critique of the limits of industrial society.

As much as certain themes in the Green movement resemble the traditions of the German intellectual Right, they are far closer in spirit to the European Left of the 19th century. Of all the types of leftist political movements of this era, the one that most resembles the political style and philosophy of the Greens is anarchism. According to G. D. H. Cole, there were two types of anarchists in the 19th century: the "individualists"

---

[4]Klemens von Klemperer, *Germany's New Conservatism: Its History and Dilemma in the Twentieth Century* (Princeton, N.J.: Princeton University Press, 1957), p. 171.
[5]*Ibid.*, p. 178.

who wanted to abolish all forms of social organization, and the "collectivists" who "combined opposition to the State as a coercive agency with a strong belief in the virtues of non-coercive association."⁶ The major assumption of the "collectivists," of whom Michael Bakunin and Peter Kropotkin were the most illustrious representatives, is that society is natural to man, and that whatever evil exists in the world is solely the result of some form of coercion. Unlike Marxists, anarchists thought of the collective in local and associative terms. They considered the state to be inherently coercive, and, like the Greens would do a century later, they combined the idea of fundamental opposition to state authority with a theory of free-association in which, according to Cole, "small local or functional units would group themselves at need for common action."⁷ The "collectivist" anarchists were, in this respect, the founders not only of the Greens' idea of "fundamental opposition" but of their concept of *Basisdemokratie* (direct democracy organized at the grass roots level) as well.

Other leftist forerunners of the Greens were the utopian socialists and, to a lesser degree, the Marxists. The utopian socialists of the early 19th century, of whom the most prominent were Charles Fourier, Robert Owen and Henri Saint-Simon, were the idealist precursors to Marx and his strictly materialist conception of socialism. Unlike Marx, who based his concept of communism on the spirit of class-solidarity, the utopian socialists appealed to the brotherhood of man and never thought of socialist organization in class terms. Their aim was to promote the general happiness of mankind by cultivating good will and cooperation, which implied neither working-class revolution nor violent opposition to the state. As the Greens would believe 150 years later, the utopian socialists maintained that proper social organization and control by producers over social affairs were sufficient to bring about a new world of international peace and human cooperation. They were critical of laissez-faire individualism and the competitive spirit of capitalism, and, by putting their faith in collective organization, they foreshadowed the very heart of socialist thinking for more than a century to come. As will be shown shortly, Marxism as a critical tool is used by a minority in the Green movement; but the Greens as a whole, with their utopianism and principle of local organization, hark back far more to the spirit of utopian socialism than to Marxism.

---

⁶G. D. H. Cole, *Socialist Thought: Marxism and Anarchism, 1850-1890* (New York: MacMillan, 1964), p. 337.
⁷*Ibid.*, p. 340.

The legacies of the Left inherited by the Greens are more European than German, but there is one last antecedent to the Green movement that is distinctively German in its cultural and political outlook—the German youth movement at the turn of the 20th century. Founded in the 1890s, the *Wandervogel* (Bird of Passage) was the first youth movement in Germany organized on a large scale. It was part of a general neo-romantic revival at the end of the 19th century, which marked the reawakening of an interest in folk culture, romantic poetry, and the heroic epics of Germany's medieval past. The *Wandervogler* celebrated the virtues of a cultural German nationalism, but they had little use for the official Prussian nationalism of the Wilhelmine Empire. The spirit of the *Wandervogel* was one of cultural revolt—revolt against bourgeois materialism as well as statist nationalism.

After World War I, the German youth movement took a decidedly sharp turn to the political Right, thereby dropping its disdain for authority and its contempt for social conformism, but before this time it had been distinctly anti-status-quo. But whether before or after World War I, the German youth movement remained hostile to the materialist values of industrial society. Like the Greens today, who command a large following among the young, the enthusiasts of Germany's first youth movement renounced bourgeois materialism because they believed it lacked idealism, depth of feeling, and the spontaneity of youth.

### Postwar Trends of Discontent in West Germany

Political discontent in West Germany in the 1950s centered largely on the national, political and security implications of Chancellor Konrad Adenauer's policy of integrating the Federal Republic into the West. The SPD's (Social Democratic Party) opposition to Western integration stemmed from the belief that such a policy would not only keep the German nation permanently divided, but would also hinder the SPD's aim of building a democratic socialist system in West Germany. The SPD was convinced that an overly close embrace of the West would serve only to strengthen the capitalist system that many of its leaders held responsible for the rise of Nazism. The security implications of Western integration caused even more unrest in the SPD. The decision to join NATO, which entailed rearmament, and the debates over the deployment of nuclear weapons in West Germany unleashed a wave of parliamentary and extra-parliamentary opposition from the SPD. The Social Democrats became leaders of the peace movements that grew out of these debates (the anti-NATO "Paul's Church Movement" and the antinuclear "Fight Against Atomic Death"), primarily because they believed that throwing West Germany firmly into the Western military camp would destroy the cause of national unity and even further strengthen the hand of Adenauer and what they considered to be his antisocialist "CDU state."[8]

Whereas the majority of the SPD leaders in the 1950s were committed to achieving the party's aims mainly by parliamentary methods, a minority in the party's left wing and in the socialist intelligentsia were not. Union activists such as Theodor Pirker and socialist intellectuals such as Franz Neumann and Wolfgang Abendroth did not share the moderate SPD leadership's willingness to work within the system to bring socialist change.[9] They disapproved of cooperating with the political system, which implied a rejection of parliamentary democracy; and, along with other socialist intellectuals and left-wing members of the SPD, they supported some form of accommodation to the East German United Socialist Party of Germany *(Sozialistische Einheitspartei Deutschlands/SED)*. Many socialists denounced the anticommunism of SPD party leaders Kurt Schumacher and Erich Ollenhauer as playing into the hands of Adenauer's Western integration policies. Foreshadowing the Greens, they considered anti-Soviet-communism to be a "restorationist" ideology designed to mobilize the masses against social progress.[10]

There are, in fact, three major legacies of the Left's battles with Adenauer in the 1950s that were bequeathed, in modified form, to the 1960s' student movement and to the Greens in the late 1970s. First, there was the tradition of antiparliamentarianism. Extra-parliamentary opposition in the 1950s, concentrated mainly in the peace movements, was based not only on the assumption that civil disobedience was a legitimate form of popular protest, but also on the radical socialist belief that the Bundestag was an illegitimate tool of capitalists, special interests and the American government. Second, there was the commonly held notion in radical socialist circles that anticommunism was an ideological weapon designed primarily to combat socialists at home. This attitude, however, was not shared by SPD leaders Schumacher and Ollenhauer, who were extremely anticommunist. Third, both the moderate and radical Left suspected that American military and economic policy in West Germany was intended merely to prop up the capitalist system as a bulwark against socialism. As will be shown later in this study, leaders of the Greens frequently

---

[8]William David Graf, *The German Left since 1945: Socialism and Social Democracy in the German Federal Republic* (Cambridge, England: Oleander Press, 1976), pp. 124-25, 128, 180.

[9]*Ibid.*, pp. 124-25, 145.

[10]*Ibid.*, p. 145.

voice their suspicions of the economic motives behind the deployment of American forces in West Germany.

But before these legacies of the Left in the 1950s would reach the Greens, they first had to be filtered through the 1960s' student protest movement. The most important organization in the student rebellion of the 1960s was the German Socialist Student League *(Sozialistischer Deutscher Studentenbund)* or SDS. Its radicalization in the early 1960s was mainly a response to the steady rightward drift of the SPD after the Godesberg Program in 1959.[11] The SDS, however, became a spearhead for a much larger protest movement in the latter part of the decade: the "Extra-Parliamentary Opposition" *(Ausserparlamentarische Opposition)*, or APO, which strove to create an all-Left popular alliance to overthrow the capitalist system in West Germany. The APO picked up many ideas from their forerunners in radical socialist circles of the 1950s. Its leaders expanded on the theory and practice of extra-parliamentary opposition, and they developed an "anti-anticommunism" even more uncompromising than that of radical socialists in the previous decade. Moreover, with the advent of American involvement in the Viet Nam War, their opposition to American foreign policy in Western Europe took on a radical character that hitherto had been the exclusive earmark of the communist Left.

The ideology of the APO and the New Left, however, was far more than a mere recapitulation of old socialist ideas. Under the influence of the Frankfurt School of Marxist critical theory, the New Left created new styles of political opposition and new types of socialist theories that would be carried over into the political mentality of the Greens. Unlike the radical socialists of the 1950s, the New Left strove for a "total" revolution of all facets of life.[12] It accepted the Marcusian dictum that socialist revolution was a psychological as well as a social affair. Its aim was to raise the consciousness of the masses out of the complacency of bourgeois life and to place it on a higher plane free of thoughts of social and mental repression. The SDS, moreover, introduced ideas of spontaneity and decentralization into the organization and style of extra-parliamentary protest. "Sit-ins," "happenings" and the like were supposed to be the marks of a more humane kind of socialism that aimed not only to bring down the capitalist system in the West, but to transcend the bureaucratic socialism of the Eastern bloc as well.

---

[11]*Ibid.*, pp. 257-64. In the Godesberg Program of November 1959, the SPD no longer claimed to be a workers' socialist party, but a reformist "people's" party. Godesberg marked the SPD's passing from democratic socialism to liberal reformism. See Graf, *op.cit.*, pp. 197-203.

[12]*Ibid.*, pp. 277-78.

The New Left's cultural critique of capitalism—especially the idea that "inner" self-determination can be achieved only by avoiding the pressures of work, state authority and consumerism—survived in the 1970s not only in radical circles, but also, in various and sometimes watered-down forms, in the media and the universities. The 1970s were a time of change in the value system of many young and middle-aged West Germans.[13] Dubbed by sociologists as the post-materialist age of value transformation, the seventies witnessed a gradual decline of interest in career and work among the young and middle-aged of the middle-class and a retreat into a private sphere of personal pleasure. Turning their backs on the materialist values of the industrial age, the new post-materialist types began to discard the positive values of perfectionism, risk-taking and personal achievement. As the material base of life became more secure for an increasingly better educated and younger middle class, questions of security began to be transferred more and more into realms dealing with the quality of life. These new devotees of the post-materialist value system were prone to emphasize psychological security over material security, spontaneity over rational calculation, and togetherness over individual competition. Status symbols based on material wealth began to give way to status symbols based on self-development. The new anticonsumer asceticism of the countercultural Alternative movement, which had taken the values of post-materialism to their most extreme form, had replaced economics with culture in defining the level of social status in the community. The "Alternatives" were, through their rejection of consumerism, consciously trying to create an antimaterialist identity by ignoring the exigencies of materialist needs. Social status had become an aesthetic question of life-style, and not a socioeconomic question of wealth and/or personal achievement.

The new values associated with the quality of life and personal well-being were grist for the intellectuals' mill of political and cultural criticism. As Federal Minister for Economic Cooperation under Willy Brandt, leftist intellectual Erhard Eppler did a great deal to popularize the notion that the new challenge for social change was no longer to equalize material

---

[13]Ronald Inglehart, *The Silent Revolution: Changing Values and Political Styles Among Western Publics* (Princeton, N.J.: Princeton University Press, 1977), pp. 37-38; and Harry Tallert, *Eine grüne Gegenrevolution. Aspekte der ökologischen Bewegung* (Frankfurt am Main: Ullstein, 1980), pp. 107-9. Other important works on value transformation in West Germany are Kendall Baker, et al., *Germany Transformed: Political Culture and the New Politics* (Cambridge, Mass.: Harvard University Press, 1981); Thomas Ziehe, *Pubertät und Narziβmus. Sind Jugendliche entpolitisiert?* (Cologne: Europäische Verlagsanstalt, 1975); and Peter Kmieciak, *Wertstrukturen und Wertwandel in der Bundesrepublik Deutschland. Eine grundlagene interdisziplinären empirischer Wertforschung mit einer Sekundäranalyse von Umfragedaten* (Göttingen: Schwarz, 1977).

gains but to improve the quality of life.[14] Eppler's campaign for a more "humane" understanding of the individual and society was complemented by the new social philosophy of the Frankfurt School which, particularly in the writings of Jürgen Habermas, contained the idea that the quality of the "inner" life should be protected from the corrupting influences of consumer capitalism.[15]

The search for better ways to enjoy life, which was merely the other side of the coin in what was really a vague sense of discontent with society in general, was politically underscored by the intellectual critique of the state bureaucracy and party system in the Federal Republic. In the highly influential work, *Wohin treibt die Bundesrepublik? (Where is the Federal Republic heading?)*, Karl Jaspers charged that the state bureaucracy was a "state organ alienated from the people," and that the parties were "oligarchies" that threatened West Germany with a new dictatorship.[16] Similarly, in *Herrschaft der Verbände (The Reign of the Federations)*, Theodor Eschenburg said much the same thing about interest organizations in the Federal Republic, calling them "duchies" that ruled the state without any regard for the general interest of the people.[17] This longing for a politics in the "general interest," for a suprapolitical communal ideal in which interest politics played no part, was an important attitudinal seed of the environmentalist movement in West Germany. It not only satisfied the need for a cause that seemed to stand above the political fray (and was therefore incapable of being refuted by politically interested arguments), it also provided a convenient outlet for the more radical post-materialists to attack the very foundations of materialist civilization.

The rise of the ecological critique of economic growth was a byproduct of post-materialist doubts about the efficacy and implications of materialist civilization. Skepticism about the feasibility of sustaining long-term economic growth first surfaced in the early 1970s in the United States and Great Britain, but it soon spread to the Federal Republic as well. Works such as Dennis and Donella Meadows' *The Limits of Growth*

---

[14]Peter Cornelius Mayer-Tasch, *Die Bürgerinitiativbewegung: Der aktive Bürger als rechts und politikwissenschaftliches Problem* (Reinbek bei Hamburg: Rowohlt, 1976), p. 24f. Particularly influential on Eppler's thought was Jay W. Forrester's *World Dynamics* (Cambridge, Mass.: Wright-Allen, 1971).

[15]Jürgen Habermas, *Theorie des kommunikativen Handelns*, vol 2: *Zur Kritik der funktionalistischen Vernunft* (Frankfurt am Main: Suhrkamp, 1981), p. 470ff. Also see Habermas, et al., *Student und Politik. Eine soziologische Untersuchung zum politischen Bewuβtsein Frankfurter Studenten* (Berlin: Luchterhand, 1969).

[16]Karl Jaspers, *Wohin treibt die Bundesrepublik? Tatsachen, Gefahren, Chancen* (Munich: Piper, 1966), pp. 114, 141-47.

[17]Theodor Eschenburg, *Herrschaft der Verbände?* (Stuttgart: Deutsche Verlag-Anstaltung, 1955), pp. 32, 64.

(1972), Barry Commoner's *The Closing Circle* (1971), and E. F. Schumacher's *Small is beautiful* (1973), had a tremendous impact on the critical intellectual community in West Germany.[18] These studies not only opened up new vistas for the economic critique of industrial capitalism, they addressed a growing concern among Europeans in general about the problems of overpopulation and pollution on a crowded continent. Their most important contribution to the ecological movement, however, was that they provided theoretical models for a comprehensive assault on the notion of economic progress. Coming, as they did, at the end of a period of sustained and rapid economic growth, these prophets of the new age of limits reflected the sense of future shock which resulted from the energy crisis, and they answered a heartfelt need of many a political activist for finding an alternative to the seemingly endless competition-game of democratic pluralism. As will be demonstrated in this study, the watchwords of the American and British pioneers in ecological thinking—"the limits of growth," "small is beautiful," "decentralization," "ecological balance" and the like—became something much more than theoretical models in the hands of the Greens. They became political slogans.

There were many *philosophes* of the ecological enlightenment in West Germany. In the latter part of the 1970s, the intellectual world and the media bustled with new ecological theories and with the names of new ecological theorists. Important among the latter was Carl Amery, who in his book *Natur als Politik* (1978) *(Nature as Politics)* warned of an ecological Armageddon if the industrial world continued on its course of exponential growth.[19] Less apocalyptic was Joseph Huber, who in *Technokratie und Menschlichkeit* (1978) *(Technology and Humanity)* explored the by now familiar proposition that technology becomes harmful to humanity if left uncontrolled.[20] The development of ecological thought had reached such a point by the late seventies that internal divisions began to emerge. Whereas Nobel Prize winner Carl Friedrich von Weizsäcker declared that industrial society had entered a new "ascetic" phase

---

[18]Dennis Meadows, et al., *The Limits of Growth* (New York: Universe Books, 1972); Barry Commoner, *The Closing Circle: Nature, Man and Technology* (New York: Knopf, 1971); and E. F. Schumacher, *Small is beautiful: A Study of Economics as if People Mattered* (London: Blond & Briggs, 1973); also see Fred Hirsch, *The Social Limits to Growth* (London: Routledge and Kegan Paul, 1977).

[19]Carl Amery, *Natur als Politik. Die Ökologische Chance des Menschen* (Reinbek bei Hamburg: Rowohlt, 1978), pp. 12ff.

[20]Joseph Huber, *Technokratie und Menschlichkeit. Zur Theorie einer humanen und demokratischen Systementwicklung* (Achberg: Achberger Verlag, 1978). Huber has recently become critical of ecological extremists; for this viewpoint, see *Die vorlorene Unschuld der Ökologie* (Frankfurt am Main: Fischer, 1982). A book that was very influential on the antinuclear energy campaign was Robert Jungk's *Der Atom-Staat. Vom Fortschritt in die Unmenschlichkeit* (Munich: Kindler, 1977).

of shortages that called for strict conservation of resources, the leftist Klaus Traube, who saw Weizsäcker's theory of asceticism as a confidence-trick to save capitalism, insisted that only socialization of the economy and absolute equality could create the conditions for an ecologically sound society.[21]

Leftist intellectuals of various political stripes were active in the West German ecological movement in the 1970s. The East German expellees Rudolf Bahro and Wolfgang Harich were at the forefront of efforts to create an updated, ecological version of Marxist critical theory.[22] The socialist Ossip K. Flechtheim, on the other hand, eschewed Marxism and harked back to the utopian socialist tradition in his attempts to build a new "ecological socialist" theory.[23] Also influential in the ecological movement was Ivan Illich, a Latin American theologian and German professor.[24] Illich's attacks on the course of industrialization in the Third World and his thoroughgoing critique of the idea of progress were to leave a lasting impression on the way the Greens have interpreted North-South relations. More politically than intellectually influential on the ecological movement was Erhard Eppler, a prominent leader of the SPD's left wing.[25] Eppler's attempt since the early part of the 1970s to introduce a quality-of-life-utopianism into social democratic thinking was instrumental in creating the political climate for the defection of many left-wing Social Democrats to the Greens in the latter part of the decade. The degree to which Eppler sympathizes with the ecological movement is evident to

---

[21]Carl Friedrich von Weizsäcker, "Gehen wir einer asketischen Weltkultur entgegen?," *Merkur* 8 (1978), pp. 745-69. Cf. Klaus Traube, *Wachstum oder Askese? Kritik der Industrialisierung von Bedürfnissen* (Reinbek bei Hamburg: Rowohlt, 1979), pp. 57-116.

[22]See Rudolf Bahro's statements at the Greens' party conference in Offenbach on November 3, 1979 in *Frankfurter Rundschau*, November 7, 1979; also see Tallert, *op.cit.*, pp. 12-15; compare with views in Rudolf Bahro, *Die Alternative. Zur Kritik des real existierenden Sozialismus* (Cologne: Europäische Verlagsanstalt, 1977), pp. 485-86. For Harich's ideas, see Wolfgang Harich, *Kommunismus ohne Wachstum? Babeuf und der "Club of Rome," Sechs Interviews mit Freimut Duve und Brief an ihn* (Reinbek bei Hamburg: Rowohlt, 1975), p. 8ff.

[23]Ossip K. Flechtheim, Der Ökosozialismus und die Hoffnung auf den neuen Menschen," in Wilfried Heidt, editor, *Abschied vom Wachstumswahn. Ökologischer Humanismus als Alternative zur Plünderung des Planeten* (Achberg: Achberger Verlag, 1981), p. 137ff.

[24]Ivan Illich, *Fortschrittsmythen. Schöpferische Arbeitslositkeit Energie und Gerechtigkeit wider die Verschulung*, Thomas Lindquist, translator (Reinbek bei Hamburg: Rowohlt, 1978), p. 7ff; also see Ivan Illich, *Selbstbegrenzung. Tools for Conviviality* (Reinbek bei Hamburg: Rowohlt, 1975).

[25]Erhard Eppler, "Faith and Science in an Unjust World," in *Report of the World Council of Churches' Conference on Faith, Science and the Future*, vol. 1: *Plenary Presentations*, Robert L. Shinn, editor; vol. 2: *Reports and Recommendations*, Paul Albrecht, editor (Geneva: World Council of Churches, 1980); also see Erhard Eppler, *Die tödliche Utopie der Sicherheit* (Reinbek bei Hamburg: Rowohlt, 1983), pp. 207-20.

this day: He has become an energetic supporter of the idea of a Green-SPD parliamentary alliance.

## From the Student Movement to the Rise of the Greens

On March 21, 1970, the executive committee of the SDS officially announced that it was dissolving its organization. Thus was the end of the political group that had been the steam engine of the West German student movement of the 1960s. The student rebellion had begun in the early sixties as an outgrowth of the leftist politics and peace movements of the previous decade; but by 1969, with the rise of the New Left and the spread of political violence, it had acquired a new character not imagined by the socialist theorists of the 1950s. The growing radicalization of the student movement in the late sixties had been the primary cause of its downfall. Student leaders had discovered that it was impossible to mobilize a mass following behind what was essentially a student revolutionary movement. The APO collapsed under the sheer weight of its overreaching goal of worldwide socialist revolution and because of the internal strife that arose from factional competition within the movement for the banner of correct theoretical socialism. Most radical student leaders of the APO generation had learned two painful lessons from their experiences in the student rebellion: never again launch a protest movement without a potential mass following, and avoid the internal dissension that results when socialist theory is given a higher priority than political praxis.

The lessons of the failed student rebellion were not lost on the leaders of the citizens' initiative movement *(Bürgerinitiativbewegung)* that emerged in the early 1970s. During this period, many ex-student leaders of the APO gave up their drive for socialist revolution and began to limit themselves to a new form of political protest, the citizens' initiative. Josef Leinen of the Federal Union of Environmental Citizens' Initiatives has defined the citizens' initiative as a "spontaneous, locally limited political action fixed on a specific goal, an action that is ceased as soon as it has either succeeded or failed."[26]

The first citizens' initiatives had actually begun during the heyday of the student movement. Local political action groups had been organized in the Ruhr district as early as 1965, and in 1967 students in Munich had combined demonstrations and self-help actions to protest an increase of fares for public transportation.[27] But the citizens' initiatives movement did

---

[26]Jo Leinen, "Von der Bürgerinitiative zur Partei?," in Petra Kelly and Jo Leinen, editors, *Prinzip Leben, Ökopax—die neue Kraft* (Berlin: Olle & Wolter, 1982), p. 115.

[27]Mayer-Tasch, *op.cit.*, pp. 10-11; and Peter Mosler, *Was wir wollten, was wir wurden. Studentenrevolte—zehn Jahre danach* (Reinbek bei Hamburg: Rowohlt, 1977), p. 269.

not really get underway until 1970-1972. During this time political initiatives against environmentally questionable urban projects and increases in public transportation fares began to spring up all over West Germany.[28] The first antinuclear energy citizens' initiative (called the "Working Circle against Radioactive Contamination") was launched in Bremen in 1972.[29] In 1974 the first coordinating committee for antinuclear energy initiatives, the "Coastal Citizens' Action" *(Bürgeraktion-Küste),* was established to coordinate the activities of 110 independent antinuclear energy political action groups in northern Germany.[30] The extent to which the political objectives of this new social protest movement had been localized was revealed clearly in a poll taken in 1972 by a research group at the Free University of Berlin: 64 percent of the citizens' initiatives examined were confined exclusively to local political issues, whereas only 23 percent were organized on a broader, regional level.[31]

The leaders of the citizens' initiative movement, many of whom were former APO leaders, not only had adopted new tactics to achieve micropolitical goals, but had embraced new themes of protest as well.[32] Former APO leaders involved in this new movement were no longer primarily interested in socialist theory, as the SDS had been, but rather in more practical problems, such as the price of public transportation, environmentalism, and, increasingly, nuclear energy. None of these issues was easily addressed at the time by either classical or New Left Marxist theory. New ecological theories imported largely from the United States provided a far better theoretical model for challenging industrial capitalism and the welfare system than Marxism. Many former APO leaders began to recognize that opposition to the political system could be built on a much broader basis if they downplayed socialist theory (or left it out altogether) and emphasized issues that related to environmentalism and improving the quality of life. There was, in fact, already a great protest potential in this area. In 1969, the Wickert Institution had discovered that 68 percent of the men and 50 percent of the women questioned in a public survey were dissatisfied with the style and workings of the state bureaucracy.[33] Environmental protection, moreover, was becoming so popular that gov-

---

[28]Mayer-Tasch, *op.cit.,* pp. 9, 11-13.

[29]Peter Willers, "Vom auf und ab der 'Grünen Liste' in Bremen," in Mettke, *Die Grünen,* p. 160.

[30]*Ibid.,* p. 161.

[31]Forschungsgruppe der Frei Universität Berlin, "Zur Rolle und Funktion von Bürgerinitiativen in der Bundesrepublik und West-Berlin. Eine Analyse von 61 Bürgerinitiativen," *Zeitschrift für Parlamentsfragen* 4 (1973), p. 268.

[32]Mayer-Tasch, *op.cit.,* p. 11f.

[33]*Ibid.,* p. 41.

ernments all over Western Europe were beginning to organize entire ministries dedicated exclusively to environmental concerns.

The real attraction of environmentalism and antinuclearism for the political activist, then, was that they represented forms of protest free of left-right ideology. For the many former APO activists involved in citizens' initiatives against nuclear reactors and polluted rivers, this was a welcome alternative to the internecine warfare over ideology that had torn the student movement apart. But there was a consequence which ex-student leaders perhaps had not envisioned: The more non-left-right issues came to dominate the citizens' initiative movement, the more populist and "bourgeois" it became. Thus, along with the broadened social base came new activists not interested in the APO generation's desire to carry on the old struggle in a different form. According to the Free University's report on the citizens' initiative movement in 1972, very few of the groups under study had ties to the extreme Left or Right.[34] This new protest movement, therefore, was by no means a mere extension of the APO. It would continue to have a leftist slant because so many of its leaders had come from the old student movement, but its objectives and its overriding philosophy had become relatively independent of the ideology and aims of the extreme organized Left.[35]

Throughout the mid-1970s the citizens' initiative movement became increasingly dominated by antinuclear energy themes. What had begun as a grass roots movement dedicated largely to environmental issues had, by 1977, become the major political vehicle for the antinuclear energy campaign in West Germany. The year 1977 was, in fact, a watershed for the antinuclear movement. The first Green electoral list, the "Green List for Environmental Protection" *(Grüne Liste Umweltschutz/GLU),* was established in Lower Saxony in 1977 by activists involved in demonstrations and citizens' initiatives against the nuclear reactors at Gorleben and Kalkar.[36] The GLU experienced a number of electoral successes at the local level in 1977. For leaders of the GLU, however, there was uncertainty whether the antinuclear movement should remain exclusively

---

[34]Forschungsgruppe der Frei Universität Berlin, *op. cit.*, p. 280.

[35]The organized Left is composed of various communist parties and organizations. The two major communist parties in West Germany are the German Communist Party *(Deutsche Kommunistische Partei/DKP),* which follows the Moscow line, and the Communist Party of Germany *(Kommunistische Partei Deutschlands/KPD),* which is Maoist. Two other organized communist groups are the Communist League *(Kommunistisches Bund/KB)* and the Communist League of West Germany *(Kommunistisches Bund Westdeutschlands/ KBW).* The undogmatic Left, as in Rudi Dutschke's case, refers to socialists unattached to the dogmas of Lenin, Trotsky or Mao.

[36]Martin Mombauer, "Die Doppelstrategie der grünen Niedersachsen," in Mettke, *Die Grünen,* pp. 135-39.

extra-parliamentary—that is, committed to mass demonstrations and acts of civil disobedience—or whether it should cultivate electoral politics and parliamentary action as the "second leg" of its opposition to nuclear energy. But electoral politics persisted in spite of these uncertainties. The following year, on June 4, 1978, the GLU showed a rather impressive 3.9 percent of the vote in the Lower Saxon state parliamentary *(Landtag)* elections, though it was not able to reach the 5 percent minimum required for parliamentary representation.[37] Not making it into parliament, however, was not a sign of total failure for the antinuclear campaign: Construction on the nuclear reactor at Gorleben had been stopped and the demonstrations had begun to attract national media attention. The GLU and "Gorleben" had become rallying points for the antinuclear energy movement in all of northern Germany.

Also important for the antinuclear energy campaign in northern Germany at this time was the "Green List" *(Grüne Liste)* in Bremen. The Green electoral list in Bremen, which in 1979 would be the first ecological/antinuclear energy initiative to achieve *Land*-level parliamentary representation in West Germany, grew out of the Coastal Citizens' Action group and the various citizens' initiatives that had been launched to protest the building of a nuclear reactor at Esenshamm.[38] Equally significant for the antinuclear energy campaign at this time were the confrontations between demonstrators and the police at the construction site for a nuclear reactor in Brokdorf in 1977.[39]

The emergence of Green lists in Bremen, Hamburg and Lower Saxony, not to mention the huge demonstrations at Brokdorf and Gorleben, had begun to attract not only the attention of the national media but the organized Left as well. In 1977-1979 there was an influx of members from the Communist League *(Kommunistisches Bund/KB)* and the Communist League of West Germany *(Kommunistisches Bund Westdeutschlands/KBW)* into the antinuclear energy movement in northern Germany.[40] In 1978 there was an organized defection of left-wing members of the SPD into the Green list in Bremen.[41] The involvement of the organized Left, however, created problems for the "pure" ecologists from the citizens' initiative movement who feared a return of the ideological battles of the APO and the domination of the antinuclear energy movement by the organized far Left. Members of the Communist League set up a separate

---

[37]*Ibid.*, p. 139.
[38]Willers, *op.cit.*, pp. 160-64.
[39]*Ibid.*, p. 165.
[40]*Ibid.*, pp. 165-66.
[41]*Ibid.*, p. 169.

electoral list *(Alternative Liste)* in Bremen to compete with Olaf Dinné's Green List, which was highly distrustful of the far Left; and the Lower Saxon GLU refused to cooperate with the Communist League-dominated "Variegated List-Defend Yourselves" *(Bunte Liste/Wehrt Euch)* in Hamburg, thus causing a split of the Alternative vote in the Hamburg communal elections in 1978.[42] Nonetheless, for all of the mutual suspicions between the "pure" ecologists and the activists from the Communist League, a significant change had come about: For the first time since the fall of the APO, the organized extreme Left was back in the business of popular protest in a major way.[43]

The reawakening of the Left was of crucial importance to the development of the ecological movement. As early as 1975, Rudi Dutschke, the ex-leader of the SDS, and Milan Horacek, an exiled dissident-socialist leader of the Prague Spring student rebellion of 1968, had discussed the prospects for forming a new "undogmatic" socialist party in West Germany.[44] Their goal was to establish a new socialist party independent of the existing ultra-leftist groups which reflected the ossified ideological battle lines of the APO generation. The relative success of the GLU at the polls in Lower Saxony in 1977 and the growing popular mood against nuclear energy eventually convinced Dutschke and Horacek to explore new ways to capture the burgeoning ecological/antinuclear movement for the cause of the Left.

Their endeavors, however, began in a most curious fashion. In 1976-1977 they started to develop ties with ultra-conservative ecological groups such as August Haußleiter's "Action Community for the Independent German" *(Aktionsgemeinschaft Unabhängiger Deutscher/AUD),* the nationalist-ecological Achberger circle, and the equally nationalistic "Action of the Third Way" *(Aktion Dritter Weg/ADW)*—all of which cultivated an anticapitalist spirit and an equal disdain for East (Soviet-style communism) and West (industrial capitalism).[45] The reasons these two

---

[42]Milan Horacek, "Zwischen uns und den Etablierten liegen Welten," in Mettke, *Die Grünen,* p. 124; and Thomas Langer and Rainer Link, "Ein Ausgangspunkt, zwei Wege—über den Umgang mit Defiziten linker Politik in Hamburg," *Alternative Stadtpolitik. Grüne, rote und bunte Arbeit in den Rathaüsern,* Reiner Schiller-Dickhut, et al., editors (Hamburg: VSA-Verlag, 1981), pp. 134-35.

[43]For a discussion of the Left's motives for entering the Green movement, see Tallert, *op.cit.,* pp. 38-41; Herbert Kitschelt, "Parlamentarismus und ökologische Opposition," in Roland Roth, editor, *Parlamentarisches Ritual und politische Alternativen* (New York: Campus-Verlag, 1980), pp. 101-2; and Andreas Buro, "Historische Erfahrungen und außerparlamentarische Politik," in *Die eigentliche Kernspaltung. Gewerkschaften und Bürgerinitiativen im Streit um die Atomkraft* (Darmstadt: Luchterhand, 1978), p. 33.

[44]Horacek, *op.cit.,* pp. 121-22.

[45]*Ibid.,* pp. 122-24.

former student leaders from the 1960s decided to open up to the far Right in the ecological movement were threefold: (1) the AUD had been the first political group to develop an ecological socialist program in West Germany (though it stood well within the conservative revolutionary tradition of the far Right); (2) the ultra-conservative ecologists were espousing a socialist and nationalist philosophy of the "third way" between communism and capitalism, which appealed to Dutschke's and Horacek's sense of wanting to transcend the left-right battles of the 1960s, not to mention their respective nationalist sensibilities; and (3) they imagined that cooperation with a "new" ecological Right dedicated to the downfall of the industrial capitalist system might improve the chances for the ecological movement to gain support for a new form of anticapitalist revolt among conservative segments of the population.

These contacts between the extreme "undogmatic" Left and the ecological far Right became the seed for the subsequent rise of the first supraregional Green election list in West Germany. In the autumn of 1977, a group of conservative ecologists and leftists met at a conference in Vlotho to coordinate the activities of the ecological movement, and, in particular, to explore the possibility of reaching a compromise between its left and right wings.[46] Present at the Vlotho conference were, among others, August Haußleiter of the AUD, the radical artist Joseph Beuys, the GLU from Lower Saxony, Wilfried Heidt of the Achberger Circle, CDU member Herbert Gruhl, Horacek, and ecologist Ossip K. Flechtheim. Out of this meeting came a series of strategy sessions and position papers on the prospects of forming a united "ecological list" for the European Parliament elections scheduled for 1979. A committee to coordinate electoral activities was set up in Troisdorf in 1978, but it was unable to head off a growing split between the conservatives and the Left, which by this time included many activists from the Communist League, the KPD and the Socialist Office *(Sozialistisches Büro/SB)*. "Undogmatic" leftists such as Horacek and Dutschke—that is, leftists with no organizational ties to the established far Left—continued with their efforts to build an ecological alliance "from Gruhl to Dutschke," but they were unable to prevent the splitting of the Green ticket between left and right wings in the Hessian state parliamentary elections in October 1978.[47]

A compromise was finally reached at a strategy conference in Frankfurt-Sindlingen in 1979. The participants at this conference put together a unified Green list for the European Parliament elections, dubbed "An Alternative Political Union: the Greens" *(Sonstige Politische Vereinigung*

---

[46]*Ibid.*, p. 124.
[47]*Ibid.*, pp. 125-26.

[SPV] *Die Grünen),* and elected an executive committee headed by Gruhl, Haußleiter and Neddermeyer of the GLU.⁴⁸ Among the candidates for the Greens were Petra Kelly, formerly of the SPD, the ultra-conservative peasant philosopher Baldur Springmann, Joseph Beuys, Ossip K. Flechtheim, theologian and peace activist Helmut Gollwitzer, and author Heinrich Böll. The Greens were heavily represented by the ultra-conservative ecologists, revealed by Gruhl's and Haußleiter's hold on two of the three seats of the executive committee; and there was a notable absence in the coordinating committees and election lists of members of the Communist League and the KPD—that is, the organized far Left. The Left in the Greens was, for the most part, of the nationalist, "undogmatic" variety, many of whom, like Rudi Dutschke, Rudolf Bahro and Milan Horacek, were expellees from the Eastern bloc. Also involved were activists from the intellectual left wing of the SPD and veterans of the antinuclear citizens' initiative movement. All in all, the Greens had reached a new stage in electoral politics. They may not have been able to achieve Rudolf Bahro's dream of an "historical compromise" between Left and Right (for the organized far Left still remained outside the Greens' purview), but they did manage to gain 3.2 percent of the West German vote for the European Parliamentary elections in 1979.⁴⁹ This was a significant figure for an electoral alliance that stood completely outside the established party system and the traditional Left-Right political spectrum.

Although the Greens were not yet a federal party—they were, on the contrary, a loose-knit electoral alliance which by no means included all of the Green lists in the Federal Republic—they had nonetheless taken a step in that direction.⁵⁰ Shortly after the European Parliament elections, the consolidating trend begun by the Greens was finally consummated in Karlsruhe on January 13-14, 1980: Delegates from all over West Germany assembled to found a full-fledged federal party—"The Greens" *(Die Grünen)*—with the intention of participating in elections at all levels of West German public life.⁵¹

Divisions between conservatives and leftists broke out almost immediately after the Karlsruhe conference. At a party assembly in Saarbrücken, a debate over double-party membership threatened to end in a dead-

---

⁴⁸*Ibid.,* p. 126.

⁴⁹*Ibid.,* p. 127.

⁵⁰Horst Bieber, Michael Schwelien and Gerhard Spörl, "Deutschland soll ergrünen," *Die Zeit,* September 10, 1982, p. 12.

⁵¹Horacek, *op. cit.,* p. 128; Tallert, *op. cit.,* p. 11; and Manuel Kiper, "Vom Umweltschutzprogramm zur Machtfrage: Die Grünen als etablierte Partei?," in Gerd Michelsen, *Öko-Politik—aber wie? Ergänzungsband zu "Der Fischer Öko-Almanach 82/83"* (Frankfurt am Main: Fischer, 1983), p. 167.

lock.[52] The conservatives, under Gruhl and Springmann, wanted to forbid dual membership because they feared that cadres from the Communist League and other far Left organizations might take over the Greens for their own purposes. Rudolf Bahro, on the other hand, welcomed the far Left into the Greens, and therefore dual membership as well, because he believed that only a "Red-Green" alliance could form the basis of a vital, new mass movement.[53] The conservatives, moreover, advocated belt-tightening measures and cutbacks in industrial production, whereas leftist delegates demanded the equalization of income for all classes and a 35-hour work week.[54] Except for dual membership, which was set aside for the time being, almost all of the leftist demands on social issues were incorporated into the Greens' party program. In spite of this rebuff, the conservative Gruhl stayed with the Greens until after the Bundestag elections in October 1980. Shortly thereafter, however, he left the Greens in protest over what he perceived to be a rising influence of the far Left on the Greens' political direction. He eventually formed his own party, the Ecological Democratic Party *(Ökologisch-Demokratische Partei)*, which Springmann and other conservative ecologists joined within the next two years.[55]

After Gruhl's defection, the Greens as a federal party took on a new face. Unlike the European Parliament Green alliance, which had been dominated by conservative ecologists and national "undogmatic" leftists, the new Green Party without Gruhl was largely composed of veterans of the antinuclear citizens' initiative movement, ex-members of the intellectual left-wing of the SPD, and activists from the organized far Left (mostly from the Communist League and the KPD). Some conservatives remained in the Greens after Gruhl's departure, but they were not nearly as powerful as before. Olaf Dinné's relatively conservative Green List for Bremen, for instance, did not join the federal Green Party, choosing to work more closely with Gruhl and Springmann instead.

Before proceeding to a discussion of the regional variations in the Green Party, it is necessary first to understand the Greens' relationship with the

---

[52]Tallert, *op. cit.*, pp. 11-12.

[53]*Ibid.*, p. 43.

[54]Kiper, *op. cit.*, p. 167.

[55]Gruhl first formed the Ecological Democratic Party in Bavaria in September 1981. It was a union of his old organization, "Action for a Green Future," conservative elements from the Lower Saxon-based "Green List for Environmental Protection," and a group called "Action Community for Ecological Policy." The first major party conference was held on March 6-7, 1982, at which the "Green List for Hamburg" merged with the Ecological Democratic Party; "Grüne dissidenten gründen Ökologisch-Demokratische Partei," *Süddeutsche Zeitung*, March 5, 1982.

33

peace movement. It was not the Greens but the Federal Union of Environmental Initiatives *(Bundesverband Bürgerinitiativen Umweltschutz/BBU)* that first expanded the antinuclear energy campaign to include opposition to nuclear weapons. The BBU was the umbrella organization for the environmentalist/citizens' initiative movement prior to the rise of the Green Party. Today it exists separate from the Greens as a union of citizens' initiative groups that prefer to stay out of party politics. Although the BBU had discussed the prospects of fusing ecological (antinuclear energy) and peace (antinuclear weapons) themes as early as 1978, it was not until after the NATO double-track decision of December 12, 1979 (which stipulated that NATO would go ahead with plans to deploy new American Pershing II and cruise missiles in Western Europe while trying simultaneously to reach an arms agreement with the Soviet Union) that it began to shift its attention primarily to the peace movement.[56]

The BBU's new emphasis on opposing nuclear weapons was carried over into the Green Party after its formation in 1980. The Greens and the BBU, along with several other groups, cooperated in formulating the "Krefeld Appeal" on November 15-16, 1980, a widely supported petition directed solely against the NATO double-track decision.[57] The Greens and the BBU worked together as well (along with Protestant peace groups) in preparing for the huge peace demonstration in Bonn on October 10, 1981, and again for the peace demonstration held the following year in Bonn on June 10, 1982.[58] Since the rise of the peace movement, the BBU has concentrated more on opposing nuclear weapons than on ecological issues, giving up much of its activities in the latter area to the Greens, but it still remains committed in principle to the combined program of ecology and peace. Whereas the BBU remains most active at the grass roots level in organizing peace initiatives, the Greens have made the peace question an issue of party politics in elections. In this respect, the BBU and the Greens more or less represent the split of the citizens' initiative movement between extra-parliamentary (BBU) and parliamentary (Greens) wings, although the Greens themselves continue to support the principle of extra-parliamentary action.

It should be clear that the Greens are a relatively loose-knit party made up of many different political types. The political variations within the

---

[56]Jo Leinen, "Wie sich die Ökologiebewegung zur Friedensbewegung erweiterte," in Kelly and Leinen, *Prinzip Leben,* pp. 16-19.

[57]Günther Schmid, *Sicherheitspolitik und Friedensbewegung, Der Konflikt um die 'Nachrüstung'* (Munich: Günter Olzog Verlag, 1982), p. 96. Also involved in the "Krefeld Appeal" was the German Communist Party.

[58]*Ibid.,* pp. 97, 99.

Green Party can best be seen at the regional level where many of the factional disputes at the national level begin, and where sometimes their outcome is determined.

One of the most important regional groups in the Green movement is the one in Hamburg, which has had an extreme leftist orientation from the very beginning of its political life. In early 1980, a Communist League contingent in the Hamburg Green alliance—the "Variegated List/Defend Yourselves"—tried to take over the city's Green movement by pushing through a militant program that was practically identical to that of the Communist League.[59] Their opponents, who were mostly environmentalist activists from the citizens' initiative movement, were shut out of the Hamburg Green alliance for a time because they wanted to join the less radical, federated Green Party organized in Karlsruhe. The schism between radicals and moderates continued until 1982, but differences were eventually set aside to build a new Green alliance—the "Green Alternative List" (Grüne-Alternative Liste/GAL)—in time for the Hamburg communal elections of June 6, 1982. In these elections the GAL leaped over the 5 percent minimum required for parliamentary representation and into Hamburg's city hall—a victory which not only locked out the Free Democratic Party (FDP), but also gave the Greens the ability to block a majority government.[60]

The new Green alliance in Hamburg, however, was still comprised largely of defectors from the organized extreme Left. Of the eight Green delegates in Hamburg's city council, three were former members of the Communist League, one was from the German Communist Party, one from the women's movement, and two from the environmentalist citizens' initiative movement.[61] Thomas Ebermann, a spokesman for the Green faction and advocate of cooperation with the SPD, has claimed that he still sees himself and the Greens as standing in the Leninist tradition.[62] But this does not mean that he supports an alliance with the German Communist Party. At a Green rally in Mainz before the Bundestag elections in March 1983, Ebermann said that working with the German Communist Party in specific areas (such as peace initiatives) was possible and even desir-

---

[59]Langer and Link, op. cit., pp. 129-34.
[60]Bieber, op. cit., p. 12.
[61]"Ohne die Grünen geht nichts," Stern, 25 (1982), pp. 67-69.
[62]"Kompromiβfähigkeit ist kein Lernziel. Spiegel Gespräch: Hamburger GAL-Abgeordnete Regula Schmidt-Bott und Thomas Ebermann über Zusammenarbeit mit der SPD," Der Spiegel, 39 (1982), p. 40.

able, but he hastily added that an alliance across the board was out of the question.[63]

Also left-radical in their orientation are the Greens in the state of Hesse. The Hessian Greens grew out of the protest movement against plans for extending a runway *(Startbahn-West)* at the Rhein-Main American air base. Other forerunners were the citizens' initiative movement against the proposed nuclear reactor at Biblis and the "Spontis," an anarchist student group.[64] Out of these protest movements came the elections of Green parliamentary factions in the Frankfurt city hall on March 22, 1981, and in the Hessian state parliament on September 26, 1982.[65] Both Green factions are by and large opposed to the principle of parliamentary cooperation, which puts them in the confrontational, "fundamental oppositionist" wing of the Green Party.[66] They are, accordingly, prone to staging provocative demonstrations in parliament, as when, for example, the Frankfurter faction showed up in the city council wearing gas masks to protest air pollution. Like federal Green leader Petra Kelly, they look upon all parliaments as "tribunes" in which to make propaganda for the Green movement.[67] The Hessian Greens have, moreover, worked off and on with the German Communist Party in organizing peace demonstrations and in sponsoring peace initiatives.[68] In the town council of the Hessian city of Marburg, the Green parliamentary faction has agreed to cooperate closely with the German Communist Party in and out of parliament.[69] Like the Greens in Hamburg, however, the Hessian Greens are careful not to appear too closely allied with the communists. An overly warm embrace would not only hurt their standing with the anticommunist leftists and ecologists within their own movement, but also expose them to politically damaging charges that they were being controlled by Moscow.

Whereas the Greens in Hesse and Hamburg are generally more leftist in their ideology than the rest of the movement, the Greens in the southwestern state of Baden-Württemberg are generally more conservative. The Greens in Baden-Württemberg, in fact, emerged in 1979 from a

---

[63]Green rally attended by author, Mainz, March 2, 1983.

[64]"Börner zeiht grün," *Süddeutsche Zeitung*, August 16, 1982; and Jan Kuhnert, "Die GRÜNEN im Marburger Stadtparlament," in Schiller-Dickhut, *Alternative Stadtpolitik*, p. 76.

[65]Horacek, *op. cit.*, pp. 130-31.

[66]"Hessens Grüne gegen jede Koalition," *Süddeutsche Zeitung*, August 16, 1982; and "Grüne zur Unterstützung der SPD bereit," *Süddeutsche Zeitung*, January 21, 1983. All attempts by the Greens to cooperate with the SPD in Hesse failed. The SPD was unable to form a majority government and new elections were called.

[67]Bieber, *op. cit.*, p. 12.

[68]Horacek, *op. cit.*, p. 133.

[69]Kuhnert, *op. cit.*, pp. 82-83.

coalition of largely ultra-conservative ecological organizations, namely, Gruhl's "Action for a Green Future," Haußleiter's "Action Community for the Independent German," and the nationalist "Achberger Circle."[70] Also involved in starting the Greens in this area were student leaders from the University of Tübingen, of whom the most prominent was Wolf-Dieter Hasenclever.[71] The student leaders of the Baden-Württemberg Greens were largely champions of a "back to nature" type of counterculture, an ideological disposition that allowed them to meet the ultraconservative ecologists on a philosophical middle-ground ruled by the principles of self-help, administrative decentralization and anti-industrialism.

After Gruhl's conservatives left the Green Party, anti-modern conservatism nevertheless remained quite strong in the thinking of the Green parliamentary faction in the Baden-Württemberg state parliament (which was elected in the spring of 1980).[72] Under the leadership of Hasenclever, the Green *Landtag* faction pursued an ultra-conservative education policy, sponsoring a parliamentary bill, for example, to return public education to the one-room school house.[73] It has, moreover, developed a number of "alternative" agricultural projects that, if implemented, would amount to developing a pre-industrial form of peasant farming not seen in Germany since the 19th century. Hasenclever's parliamentary faction has tried to coordinate their agricultural policy with that of a number of small-holding peasant organizations in Baden-Württemberg whose members feel threatened by agricultural modernization and the growth of big agri-business.[74] This willingness to reach out to conservative segments of the population reflects Hasenclever's goal of making the Greens a mass movement for all social classes. The Greens in Baden-Württemberg are ready to compromise with all political parties, but only if they adopt an ecological approach to economic development.[75] Other Greens in Baden-Württemberg, like Winfried Kretschmann, for example, are strong advocates of an alliance with the SPD, something which has not yet happened, but which nonetheless is a topic of intense debate in the media.

---

[70]Jörg R. Mettke, "Auf beiden Flügeln in die Höhe: Grüne, Bunte und Alternative zwischen Parlament und Straße," in Mettke, *Die Grünen*, p. 13.

[71]For Hasenclever's ideas, see Wolf-Dieter and Connie Hasenclever, *Grüne Zeiten. Politik für eine lebenswerte Zukunft* (Munich: Kösel, 1982).

[72]Mettke, *op. cit.*, p. 13.

[73]Wolf-Dieter Hasenclever, "Die Grünen im Landtag von Baden-Württemberg. Bilanz nach zwei Jahren Parlamentspraxis," in Mettke, *Die Grünen*, pp. 102-3.

[74]*Ibid.*, p. 109.

[75]Jörg Bischoff, "Die Grünen vor dem Sündenfall," *Die Zeit*, April 2, 1982.

The Greens in Baden-Württemberg are not the only regional group to have developed an anti-industrial conservative ideology and a compromising attitude toward the political system. The Greens in the northern German port town of Bremen ("Green List for Bremen") have refused to join the federated Green Party because they believe it is too closely aligned with the organized far Left. The Bremen Greens, who in October 1979 spearheaded the movement's drive for official representation by being the first Green list to enter parliament, are very much of the original citizens' initiative mold, that is, of the type that existed at the local level before the influx of activists from the organized far Left. Their leader, Olaf Dinné, is formerly of the SPD, as is another Bremen Green, Peter Willers, who has since left the "Green List for Bremen" to join the federal party.[76] Dinné's anticommunism has led him not only to shun the Greens' national leadership, but to form a political union—called the Ecological Federation *(Ökologische Föderation)*—with Gruhl and Springmann.[77] Like Hasenclever in Baden-Württemberg, Dinné envisions a broad social movement for the Greens, and in his efforts to reach out to other parties he has even made contacts with the CDU.[78]

Dinné and the Bremen Greens are, in this respect, similar to the regional Green organization in Bavaria. The Greens in both Bremen and Bavaria take the less hostile view of the conservative establishment than the majority of the movement's supporters—an outlook which arises not only from anticommunism but from an anti-industrial social conservatism. These attitudes, however, are not shared by the "alternative" ecologists in Bremen and Bavaria. Ecological activists from the far Left in Bremen will have nothing to do with Dinné, whereas the Greens in Nuremberg and Munich, many of whom are student activists out of the anarchist "Sponti" movement, shun the older, more conservative Green activists in the rural parts of Bavaria.[79] Unlike the "Green List for Bremen," the Bavarian Greens belong to the federal party. However, they have not yet achieved parliamentary representation and, along with the Greens in the Rhineland-Palatinate, are among the most organizationally weak and numerically small regional groups in the entire Green movement.

Like the Greens in Bremen, the "Alternative List for Democracy and Environmental Protection" in West Berlin, too, has not merged into the

---

[76]"In Bremen bleibt der Trend Genosse," *Vorwärts*, July 15, 1982.

[77]Willers, *op. cit.*, p. 178.

[78]Niels von Haken, "Grünes Experiment in Bremen ist gescheitert," *Vorwärts*, January 7, 1982.

[79]Willers, *op. cit.*, p. 170; and Heinz Höfl, "Ökologie in Lederhosen. Grünseim in Bayern," in Mettke, *Die Grünen*, pp. 60-61, 65-68.

federal party of the Greens.[80] Founded on October 5, 1978, this electoral alliance evolved out of West Berlin's far Left and the countercultural "alternative" scene. On May 10, 1981, it gained a significant victory in the West Berlin Senate elections (7.2%), sending nine delegates into parliament.[81] The key group in the AL's leadership is a faction made up of former members of the Maoist KPD. It has consistently been the steering faction within the alliance, and it governs with the approval of a second group composed of ex-SPD "democratic socialists" and activists from the Communist League.[82] Because the Left is so strong in the AL, ecological questions take a back seat to other issues in its political program. It is committed not only to protecting the environment, but to "democratic rights," women's issues, and union politics as well.

Strictly speaking, the West Berlin Alternative List is only a fellow-traveler of the Green-ecological movement. Its originators jumped on the ecological bandwagon because they saw it as an excellent opportunity to unite the bitterly divided and homeless Left in West Berlin.[83] As a result of the AL's leftist history, the federal party of the Greens has not been able to put its stamp on West Berlin's Alternative movement. The Greens there are largely under the thumb of the AL leadership, leaving the "Green List for Berlin" *(Grüne Liste/Berlin)*, a totally independent alliance, as the only ecological-alternative list with no close contact with the AL. The Alternatives in West Berlin are far more steeped in socialist ideology than the Green Party, and though they are willing to cooperate with the SPD in the Senate, they have close ties to West Berlin's countercultural scene, which is perhaps the most radical of its kind in West Germany.[84] Many of the AL's leaders, especially those from the organized far Left, understand the Alternative movement to be a mere middle stage in the march toward a "modern" form of socialism.[85] The new political ecology, the very intellectual substance of the Green movement, is of only secondary importance to most of the leaders of West Berlin's "Alternative List for Democracy and Environmental Protection."

### The Social and Political Composition of the Green Movement

People from all ages and political persuasions can be found in the Green Party—from the elderly who worry about their pensions and the threat of

---

[80]The German title for the AL is *Alternative Liste für Demokratie und Umweltschutz*.
[81]Hoplitschek, *op.cit.*, p. 89.
[82]*Ibid.*, pp. 83-86, 96.
[83]*Ibid.*, pp. 82, 87.
[84]*Ibid.*, p. 92. The newspaper of the alternative "scene" in West Berlin is *Die Tageszeitung*, or "taz," which is distributed outside West Berlin as well.
[85]Hoplitschek, *op. cit.*, p. 100.

nuclear war, to young "urban Indians" *(Stadtindianer)* who live in ghetto-like conditions in some of West Germany's major cities. Despite these variations, the Greens are generally a middle-class party of the young and the early middle-aged. Green voters are mostly between the ages of 18 and 30, and the Greens' leaders are for the most part in their late twenties and thirties.[86] According to *Jugend '81,* a study of West German youth commissioned by the German Shell Corporation, 20 percent of the Federal Republic's youth feel closer to the Greens than to any other party.[87] The Greens are more popular with middle-class university students than with working-class youth; and the more educated any age group is, the more likely it is to sympathize with some of the political goals of the Greens.[88]

If one looks at the poll data on youth attitudes toward the "Alternative" movement—keeping in mind that this is a broad countercultural movement in which the Greens figure as merely the most organized and largest political group—the importance of Alternative culture to students in particular becomes unmistakable: According to a study by Krause, Lehnert and Scherer, approximately 50 percent of West German students have "strong affinities" to Alternative culture, while between 80-90 percent show tolerant attitudes toward it.[89] Students comprise a high proportion of the membership and voting constituencies of all political groups associated with the Alternative movement—not only the Greens but also the quintessentially countercultural "Alternative List for Democracy and Environmental Protection" in West Berlin.[90]

---

[86]For figures on the age of Green voters, see Werner Harenberg, "Sicherer Platz links von der SPD? Die Wähler der Grünen in den Daten der Demoskopie," in Mettke, *Die Grünen,* p. 36.

[87]Jugendwerk der Deutschen Shell, *Jugend '81. Lebensentwürfe, Alltagskultur, Zukunftsbilder,* 3 vols. (Hamburg: Jugendwerk der Deutschen Shell, 1981), p. 16.

[88]For poll figures on the relation of education to sympathy for the Greens, see Harenberg, *op. cit.,* p. 37.

[89]Christian Krause, Detlef Lehnert and Klaus-Jürgen Scherer, *Zwischen Revolution und Resignation. Alternativkultur, politischen Grundströmungen und Hochschulaktivitäten in der Studentenschaft; Eine empirische Untersuchung über die politischen Einstellungen von Studenten* (Bonn: Verlag Neue Gesellschaft, 1980), p. 198.

[90]According to Sontheimer, every seventh member of the AL aspires to be an academic, while only around 8 percent are workers. This clearly shows the educated middle-class orientation of the Alternative movement in West Berlin. Hoplitschek has pointed out that there was a high proportion of students and public servants in education and health care among the voters for the AL in the city elections of March 1979. Michael Sontheimer, "Eine Partei, die keine Partei sein will: die AL," *Lokal 2000. Berlin als Testfall,* Heinrich Albertz, et al., editors (Reinbek bei Hamburg: Rowohlt, 1983), p. 239; also see Hoplitschek, *op. cit.,* p. 85.

Nevertheless, the majority of West German youth are neither hard-core Alternatives nor devotees of the Green Party. According to Krause et al., only 11.9 percent of West German students are devoted wholeheartedly to the life-styles and ideals of Alternative culture—that is, to rejecting all forms of authority and to disparaging the ideals of the achievement society.[91] Moreover, extrapolating from the figures in the *Jugend '81* study, we find that around 80 percent of youth as a whole do not feel particularly close to the Green movement. Although the majority of youth do indeed maintain a critical distance from the West German political system (in which the parties bear the brunt of the criticism), between 60 and 90 percent approve of the democratic system, and around 80 percent are "on the whole" satisfied with the economic system.[92] Criticism of the political system is strongest among students, but not even a majority of them are so entirely disillusioned with parliamentary democracy as to join or vote for the Greens or a far Left party. The SPD still commands the political loyalties of the largest bloc of young voters in West Germany, and the youth organizations of the other established parties retain a hold on sizable portions of the youth population as well. All in all, the potential for extra-parliamentary protest among youth is somewhere between 10 and 15 percent of those between 14 and 21 years of age.[93] One would expect a larger number of sympathizers, not only from the young but from the older generations as well.

There is no ideal social type that consistently joins or votes for the Greens, but clearly a large proportion of their political activists and voters are university students who want but cannot obtain careers in the university, secondary education or public services.[94] Jobs in these areas are exceedingly difficult to find in West Germany, and the unemployment problem for the young, educated middle-class in general is an underlying factor in the popularity of the Greens in the universities. Moreover, there is a relatively high proportion of teachers and social workers in the Greens, which is a consequence not only of job insecurity in the public sector of the economy, but of status insecurity for those who already have jobs. As part of the educated elite, these groups often feel frustrated over

---

[91]Krause, *op. cit.*, p. 203.

[92]Bundesministerium für Jugend, Familie und Gesundheit, *Jugend in der Bundesrepublik heute* (Bonn: Bundesministerium für Jugend, Familie und Gesundheit, 1981), pp. 6-7; and Jugendwerk der Deutschen Shell, *Die Einstellung der jungen Generation zur Arbeitswelt und Wirtschaftsordnung* (Hamburg: Jugendwerk der Deutschen Shell, 1980), p. 69.

[93]Roland Schmidt, "Zur alternativen Kultur. Erscheinungsbild und Strukturen," *Aus Politik und Zeitgeschichte*, March 19, 1983, p. 47.

[94]For the social make-up of the AL's voting constituency and its party membership, see Sontheimer, *op. cit.*, p. 239.

not being able to have a greater voice in shaping government policy. The Greens are, in this respect, a party that caters to the educated "new middle-class," that is, to social groups involved in one way or another in education, public administration and the service industry. By no means do the Greens command the political loyalties of the entire new middle-class—after all, the latter constitutes a huge segment of society, and the Greens received only 5.6 percent of the vote in the March 1983 Bundestag elections—but they have made inroads into it, helping to fulfill the increasing demand for more state attention to issues touching on the quality of life.

The political composition of the Green movement, like its social composition, is diverse. The so-called pure ecologists constitute the largest and most influential group within the Green Party; they are committed primarily to environmental protectionism and to developing a fundamental critique of industrial-technological civilization. Next in importance are activists and intellectuals associated either formerly or currently with the Left; there is a tendency among these "ecological socialists" to retain the "social question" of economic equality in their analysis of ecological problems, and in certain circles at least, an effort is made to combine a Marxist critique of capitalism with the ecologists' critique of technology and industrialism. A third category, which will be called here "miscellaneous alternative," is a cornucopia of reformists from the Alternative movement including such politically diverse groups as anarchists ("Anarchos" and "Spontis"), radical feminists and gay rights advocates. The "miscellaneous alternatives" have no unifying ideology, and they are not as influential as the ecologists and leftists; they are, moreover, only secondarily interested in the ecologists' critique of industrial society. Finally, similar to the "pure" ecologists in program but different in political orientation are the ultra-conservatives—sometimes called "Value Conservatives" *(Wertkonservativen)*—who, for the most part, do not belong to the Green Party. They are principally opposed to what they perceive to be the negative cultural and spiritual ramifications of industrial-technological civilization—that is, its materialism and the fragmenting effect they believe it has on the moral fabric of the community. None of these groups is mutually exclusive—there is, in reality, often a great deal of overlap among them—but they do describe in general terms the main political categories which the Greens themselves often use to distinguish factions from one another.

The primary aims of the "pure" ecologists are to raise the ecological consciousness of the population and to build economic models for a new society based on ecological principles. For, as these ecologists see it, we are standing on the brink of a new period in the history of the human race: We are facing, they insist, the unavoidable decline of industrial-technological civilization, and only the Greens, as the new party of the ecological avant-garde, can lead us out of the pre-revolutionary crisis of industrial capitalism into a future free of dirty, sprawling cities, polluted rivers and endless economic growth.[95] In this new society imagined by Green ecologists, the economy would be completely decentralized and production stripped of its current industrial function. Agriculture would be returned to the peasant farm, and the use of modern technology would be severely limited, if not eliminated altogether.[96] In addition to manufacturing ecological panaceas for the future, there is the goal of overthrowing what ecologist Carl Amery has called the "ruling explanatory system" of the contemporary industrial order.[97] This amounts to a fundamental critique of all facets of industrial capitalism: the political order, the economic system, and the culture of consumerism and technology. The actual tactics to be used in achieving this ecological revolution vary from passive resistance to playing politics within the parliamentary system, but the overall aim for the "pure" ecologists is roughly the same: to build a new social order based not on the realities of industrialism and the exigencies of "economic man," but on the potential of economic cooperation and the exigencies of nature.

Unlike the "pure" ecologists, who speak of an ecological crisis of industrialism, the ecological socialists try to expose what they perceive to be the internal ecological contradictions of "late capitalism." The most prominent spokesmen for the ecological socialists are Rudolf Bahro, Ossip K. Flechtheim, and Wolfgang Harich. Bahro and Harich are Marxists. All of these intellectuals advocate more or less a "Red-Green" synthesis of the ecologists' critique of industrialism with a socialist critique of capitalism. A persistent theme is that the decline of industrial capitalism has reached a new ecological phase in which capitalists will try to save themselves by increasing economic exploitation, political oppression, and destruction of the environment. Harich, for example, believes that only communism can avert the coming ecological disasters of late capitalism because it is, of all the world's economic systems, the most frugal.[98] Flechtheim shares Harich's faith in the frugality of socialism: Only a socialist economy, he contends, can truly accept the limits of growth and build a human society free of polluted air and dirty rivers. Bahro, on the other hand, wants to develop an eclectic and populistic form of socialism that would

---

[95]Tallert, op. cit., p. 21.

[96]For Green leader Petra Kelly's ideas on agriculture, see Petra K. Kelly, Um Hoffnung kämpfen. Gewaltfrei in eine grüne Zukunft (Bornheim-Merten: Lamuv-Verlag, 1983), pp. 133-36. For Hasenclever's ideas on agriculture, see Hasenclever, op. cit., pp. 146-55.

[97]Amery, op. cit., p. 12ff; Cf. Tallert, op. cit., pp. 116-17.

[98]Harich, op. cit., p. 8ff; Cf. Tallert, op. cit., p. 18.

encompass elements from ecology, Marxism, nationalism and, to a lesser degree, even Christianity.[99]

Marxists such as Bahro and Harich represent only a minority point of view in the Green Party, but they are influential in Green circles dominated by former members of the Communist League and other organizations from the far Left. There is, however, no ideological unity among leftists in the various parliamentary factions of the Green Party, and the concept of ecological socialism in the Green movement as a whole is more utopian than Marxist. Its most common characteristic is the tendency to lump capitalism into the overall ecological critique of industrialism, and an unwillingness to give up the "social question" in the practical work of opposing the political system.

The "miscellaneous alternatives" are much more difficult to describe than the ecological socialists or "pure" ecologists. For our purposes, they are defined as containing all followers of the Alternative movement in the Green Party who are not primarily ecologists or ecological socialists. It is important, in this respect, to realize that the Greens are merely a political subset in the Alternative movement. Although an "alternative" can be a Green, not all "alternatives" are Greens. By the same token, an "alternative" can be a leftist—indeed, in West Berlin most of them are—but a leftist is not necessarily always an "alternative." This is because the word "alternative" refers largely to culture, that is, to a countercultural life-style that can take many different political forms. Whether an "alternative" is a Green, a communist, an ecological socialist, or even an anarchist is not nearly as decisive in defining what "alternative" means as whether the subject is a practicing opponent of the life-style and values of bourgeois culture. Although the "alternatives" are mainly creatures of culture, they do have some political attitudes in common. They are, for example, generally hostile to bureaucracy and technological change, and they are deeply repulsed by consumerism and materialism.[100] Some members of the Alternative movement even go so far as to claim that consumerism is merely another form of totalitarianism.

In the end, the Alternative movement is really little more than a rallying point for the various countercultural movements that grew up in West Germany in the 1970s. Radical feminists, "Spontis," experimental therapists, gay rights advocates, and religious sectarians are merely part of a Green constituency in which the "pure" ecologists and ecological socialists predominate. As one might expect, the "miscellaneous alter-

---

[99]Tallert, *op. cit.*, pp. 12-15.
[100]Schmidt, *op. cit.*, p. 44.

natives" are not an organized political force, nor are they as a group very influential within the Greens. They are far more likely to be followers than leaders (with the exception of the feminists and, to a lesser degree, the "Spontis"), not only because they are relatively young, but because they possess no underlying political theme to unify them. Although not all "alternatives" are followers of the Green Party, they do provide the Greens with votes and with a significant level of "street support" in demonstrations and other forms of extra-parliamentary protest.

The ultra-conservative ecologists are the social opposites of the "miscellaneous alternatives." Led by Herbert Gruhl, Baldur Springmann and August Hauβleiter, the ultra-conservative ecologists can best be described as cultural counter-revolutionaries who stand well within the German tradition of revolutionary conservatism. Unhappy in the modern technological age, they want to turn the clock back to a simpler time when community ties were strong and the landscape uncluttered by superhighways and suburban sprawl. Gruhl and the ultra-conservative ecologists in the Ecological Democratic Party are attacking not only what they believe to be the crass materialism of modern times, but the de-spiritualization of society by technology and science.[101] Sounding very much like a conservative revolutionary from the early part of the century, Gruhl has portrayed the ecological movement as a "counterblow of life against the soulless mechanistic spirit of the mechanistic age."[102]

Gruhl's deputy, the "ecological peasant" *(Öko-Bauer)* Baldur Springmann, is no less worried about technology than Gruhl; he insists that only a "spiritual revolution" can save the world from ecological catastrophe.[103] By this he means that we must radically reorient our way of thinking from technology and science toward a semi-mystical and biological conception of society. Springmann wants to create a new harmony between man and nature; he wants to organize society and production along strictly natural lines. Gruhl's and Springmann's appeal for a new ecological society is complimented well by August Hauβleiter's idea of ecological socialism, a socialism, however, not of the Left, but of a "third way"

---

[101] Herbert Gruhl, *Ein Planet wird geplündert. Die Schreckensbilanz unserer Politik* (Frankfurt am Main; Fischer, 1975), pp. 245-55.

[102] Speech by Herbert Gruhl, party rally of "Action for a Green Future," Stuttgart-Böblingen, September 8, 1979; quoted from Tallert, *op. cit.,* p. 48.

[103] Baldur Springmann, *Partner Erde. Einsichten eines Öko-Bauern* (Kiel: Arendt, 1982), pp. 79-80.

between capitalism and communism.[104] Like Gruhl and Springmann, Haußleiter envisages an organic community (hence the "socialism") in which society and economy are regulated to achieve a harmony between man and nature.

These theories are not as ideologically removed from the thinking of "pure" ecologists as one might think. In spite of their different attitudes about cooperating with the far Left, both the "pure" ecologists and the ultra-conservative ecologists are fundamentally opposed to the spirit of industrial-technological civilization. Moreover, they both conceive of the ideal community in terms that imply a clear rejection of political and economic pluralism. Wolf-Dieter Hasenclever, a "pure" ecologist who worked closely with the ultra-conservatives in the early part of his career, has described the Greens as having a "clear conservative orientation."[105] But this is a conservatism not in a pragmatic political sense—for both the Left and the Right in the Green movement are opposed to the political system—but rather in a romantic and culturally revolutionary sense. The meeting of reactionary romanticism and socialist thought on a common ground is not new to German intellectual history. It was indeed quite common among conservative revolutionaries in the Weimar Republic. Whether conservative romanticism and socialist ideology in the Greens will move closer to one another in the future is uncertain, but it is a possibility that is not without precedent in the history of German political thought.

---

[104] Mettke, *op. cit.*, p. 13. In keeping with the "third way" orientation of some ecologists in the Green movement, Neo-Nazis have begun to express an interest in the ecological movement. Martin Mussgung, the chairman of the Neo-Nazi National Democratic Party, has been quoted as saying: "If a few farsighted leftists have recently seen the 'danger of a rightist development' in the 'Green wave,' we do not want to contradict them." (Quoted from Mettke, *op. cit.*, p. 15.) A number of ex-Nazis have, in fact, found their way into the Green Party. Most notable was Werner Vogel, an ex-Nazi official who has admitted to knowing about the extermination of the Jews during the Second World War. As a result of this discovery, he was forced to resign his seat in the Bundestag. "So weit zurück," *Der Spiegel*, 12 (1983), pp. 110-11. Another ex-Nazi is Gustine Johannsen, a leader of the Greens in Hamburg; "Vergangenheit als politisches Instrument," *Frankfurter Allgemeine Zeitung*, April 26, 1983, p. 2.

[105] Quoted from Mettke, *op. cit.*, p. 12.

# The Green Program for German Society and International Affairs

## by Clay Clemens

Shortly before the 1983 federal election, Social Democratic spokesman Egon Bahr declared, "I've read numerous Greens statements and talked to many of their leaders, but I still don't know what they stand for."[1] This expression of bafflement from a leading leftist has been echoed countless times by analysts representing every part of the political spectrum in West Germany. Friends, foes and neutral observers agree that the Greens' positions on most questions of policy are vague and often incoherent. Because the movement despises traditional party politics, it downplays programmatic clarity; distrusting technical expertise, it disregards practical feasibility; bored by philosophical abstractions, it places no premium on intellectual consistency; and weary of ideological rigidities, it espouses no clear worldview. As self-proclaimed representatives of popular protest, of street demonstrators and citizens action groups, the Greens instead develop their policy ideas, criticisms and objectives in accordance with different standards, such as "spontaneity" and grass roots control. Above all, the Greens insist on obeying the desires of their "basis," but as one critic remarked, "what this 'basis' is, no one seems to know; a conference is called and whoever shows up—that's the 'basis.'"[2] The difficulty of hammering out concrete policy under such circumstances as the Greens tolerate is illustrated by the remark of one delegate at a chaotic, delay-plagued conference, who said, "We have no more time and should wind up now. Anyway it has already been agreed that our program will continually change."[3]

For these reasons, as well as the fact that the Greens will never gain real political power (and, indeed, fell short of their expectations in the March 1983 federal elections), there has been a tendency among critics and

---

[1]*Akron Beacon Journal*, March 6, 1983.
[2]Dr. Werner Kaltefleiter in comments before the Institute for Foreign Policy Analysis, Cambridge, Massachusetts, May 2, 1983.
[3]*Die Zeit*, January 28, 1983, p.4.

sympathizers alike to treat Green policy positions lightly and focus instead upon the movement's origins and composition, or the party's disruptive impact upon West German politics. This study seeks to provide a more complete picture of the Green movement by taking its policy statements and policy programs seriously—perhaps even more seriously than do many members themselves.[4] Examining the Greens in light of their policy positions will help explain a great deal about the movement's character and appeal, while also determining the extent to which its views are unique or are, instead, "extreme formulations of sentiments voiced elsewhere in muted, more respectable tones."[5]

To begin, the Green critique of modern West German society and contemporary international affairs is comprehensive; almost nothing in the world about them do the Greens find acceptable. This reflects in part the movement's broad heterogeneous composition. As a coalition, an "omnibus for minorities," the Greens must address the particular gripe of each individual subgroup. But aside from its makeup, the movement is predisposed toward a negative view of the Establishment and its policies. As one satirical slogan puts it, "I'm a Green: I'm Against Everything."

As the Greens see it, Germany and the world are confronted by bleak prospects in every direction primarily because Western society is completely dominated by a "throwaway mentality" (*Wegwerfmentalität*) that is allegedly willing to dispose too easily of everything from trash to human lives. This mentality is seen as undermining the entire Western system, and thus problems proliferate: a fascination with nuclear energy leads to repressive government measures, it is said, while, to take another exam-

---

[4]Green programs form the basis of this study. Unless otherwise noted, all policy concepts attributed to the movement are drawn from *Die Grünen: Das Bundesprogramm* (hereafter cited as *BP*), the program prepared for the 1983 federal election, as well as several other documents: *Die Grünen, Landesverband Bayern: Wahlplattform '82* (hereafter cited as *Bay*), the 1982 Bavarian state-election platform; *Die Grünen, Landesverband Bayern: Energieversorgung für Bayern ohne Atomenergie und Erdol* (hereafter cited as *Bay-Energie*), the 1982 Bavarian State-election statement on "Energy Provision for Bavaria without Nuclear Power and Oil;" *Die Grünen, Landesverband Hessen: Handeln für eine lebenswerte Zukunft* (hereafter cited as *Hessen*), a 1982 Hesse state-election statement; *GAL Programm für Hamburg* (hereafter cited as *Ham*), the 1982 Green-Alternative List program for the Hamburg city elections; *Friedensmanifest: Die Grünen* (hereafter cited as *FM*), the Greens' 1983 Peace Manifesto; *Paktfreiheit für beide deutsche Staaten, Atomwaffenfreies Europa vom Atlantik Zum Ural, Einheit für Deutschland* (hereafter cited as *Pakt*), the Berlin Alternative List's statement on the national question and foreign policy. Other specific sources, including documents, speeches, articles and interviews will be cited separately.

[5]John Markham, "Germany's Volatile Greens," *New York Times*, Magazine section, February 13, 1983.

ple, war is blamed on the "expansion of industrial society, its search for profit and power."⁶

As a result of this comprehensive attitudinal and thus systemic failing, the Greens declare that all change must be fundamental; nothing less than a 180-degree shift in perspective and policy will suffice. If factions differ over the manner and timetable under which these changes must occur, all Green programs make it clear that the necessary transformation must be deep and broad. Petra Kelly put it concisely: "The 'Greens' seek a new style of living, not only in the western [world], but also in their own political worlds. They would like better, nonexploitative forms of life, alternative forms of life and nonviolent relations to others. . . ."⁷

Green ideology is characterized by four concepts, expressed in four words that have come to be the movement's slogan: ecological, social, "basis-democratic" and nonviolent. Each term is intended to highlight the flaws of the present system and point the way toward a better future; each has relevance to the discussion of domestic as well as foreign affairs. Consequently, these Green leitmotifs are broadly conceived. "Ecological" means more to the Greens than the conservation of nature, because they believe the environment must be seen as a whole, encompassing the work-place, the home, the city, and other societies, as well as the wilderness. In the Green view, man's present plight stems from an unwillingness to see that the natural and human worlds are inseparable. Growth, competition, technology and profit destroy the environment in all its dimensions, causing "the complete devastation and contamination of our life's foundations."⁸ A truly "ecological" orientation in the Green sense signifies a recognition of the need for healthy, natural surroundings and an end to the exploitation of a limited planet's natural and human resources. This, they claim, would be a society conducive to cooperative productivity and thus "qualitative growth."

Similarly, the Green concept of "social" blends some Marxist terms with certain allusions to essentially preindustrial values like *Gemeinschaft* (or community), as well as to liberal notions of personal autonomy. The unifying theme is their desire for a "new human togetherness," as opposed to the current "struggle of every man against every other man."⁹ This requires an end to the exploitation of the market both at home and abroad,

---

⁶*Bay* (Präambel, Gewaltfrei).

⁷Petra Kelly, "Das System ist bankrott—die neue Kraft muss her!," in Petra Kelly and Jo Leinen, editors, *Prinzip Leben: Ökopax—Die Neue Kraft* (Berlin: Olle & Wolter, 1982), p. 137.

⁸*Bay* (Präambel, Ökologisch).

⁹*Ibid.* (Präambel, Sozial).

to the dehumanizing division of labor, and to stifling bureaucracy, and replacing them with more decentralized, cooperative and humane structures. Petra Kelly emphasizes that the essence of the Greens' "social" goals is to make people no longer feel "superfluous"; instead, within their gender, generations and groups, they must be allowed "to realize themselves, . . . no longer in isolated, lonely solitary struggles at the cost of competition . . . but in association with others and against the *bürgerlich* coldness."[10]

*Basisdemokratisch,* or democracy from the grass roots, is the third Green leitmotif. Like the others, it encompasses a multitude of virtues. According to the movement, present German society and international relations are characterized by the concentration of economic, social and political power in the hands of stifling and uncaring oligarchies and bureaucracies. Green programs foresee "a strengthened realization of decentralized, direct democracy" giving priority to "the decisions of the basis" made in referenda, citizen-action groups, or at the lowest level of administration.

Finally, the Greens glorify nonviolence as a guiding principle for events within and outside Germany. Casting a critical eye at contemporary political, social and economic relationships, the Greens deplore repression and war, and declare that "humane goals cannot be achieved by inhumane means." Certain dominant but unnamed elements are said by the Greens to see the use of force as in their interest, and this tendency toward violence encourages "authoritarian rule, that takes on ever more dangerous dimensions."[11] The Greens see nuclear weapons as the inevitable result of this preoccupation with violence. To cleanse their own society and the outside world of this threatening power fetish, the Greens advocate a principle of nonviolence "without exception between all people, thus even within social groups and society as a whole as well as between nations and nationalities."[12]

## The Green View of German Society

### Green Criticisms of Modern German Society

In general, the Greens blame all of Germany's domestic problems on a society which they claim is more concerned with profit and a quest for prosperity than with human needs. Domestic ills, ranging from unemployment and energy scarcity to inadequate child care, can be traced to

---

[10]Kelly, "Das System ist bankrott," *op. cit.*, p. 137.
[11]*Bay* (Präambel, Gewaltfrei).
[12]*Ibid.*

the allegedly massive failure of a growth-oriented, technological, centralized, bureaucratized society and its disregard for ecological, social, "basis" democratic and nonviolent considerations.

Unemployment, for example, is seen as resulting from dependence on large-scale technology, as well as capital-intensive and energy-intensive production methods; the lack of jobs is further attributed to the omnipotence of monopolistic corporations which direct investment away from labor-intensive projects and permit little worker influence over management decisions. Under these conditions human inputs are said to become expendable, and thus there is not only unemployment, but underemployment, low wages, poor working conditions and low productivity.

According to the Green critique, each separate sector of German socio-economic life suffers from the same basic flaws. Energy scarcity (and the allegedly excessive and dangerous steps taken to solve it) is said to stem from the shortcomings of the West German system, with its all-consuming obsession with growth. Germany's large corporations and government bureaucracy have vital interests, it is said, in higher output and greater wealth to justify their monopolization of the system, and this requires expansion—and thus energy provision—far beyond the needs of people and the ecological limits of the environment. According to the Greens, Germany's present commitment to high-technological, capital-intensive, centrally-controlled atomic energy and fossil fuel production serves the system's desire for constant expansion. Nuclear power is criticized as too costly, given its security requirements, waste disposal problems, and the scarcity of uranium; fossil fuel supplies, and above all oil (opinion is divided on coal), depend on risky, greedy foreign producers and similarly involve substantial ecological costs.

Analogous problems can be found, according to the Greens, in a transportation network that emphasizes auto travel, subways and jet planes. These are reputed to be increasingly expensive because of the costs involved in mitigating their environmental damage, their disruption of traditional urban and rural social patterns, and their centralized, bureaucratic administration. In the Green view, present means of transport fail to meet local transportation requirements because of their emphasis on long-range travel. Current housing policies are also criticized because they are profit-oriented and run by the bureaucracy at the expense of ecological, social and "democratic" concerns. Large construction firms and governmental planners have a joint interest in massive commercial buildings and housing complexes which are inordinately expensive and lead to the rising homelessness and poverty accompanying overcrowded urban life.

51

German agriculture is said to suffer because farmers have been forced to leave the land, squeezed out by wage inequalities resulting from the strength of agri-business firms with their chemical fertilizers and mass-scale technologies, desire for profit, and ultimate control of the market. Provision of health care is said to be an expensive failure for familiar reasons: a system which promotes ecological destruction allegedly creates more sickness than it can cure with technology and chemical medicines; a health network controlled by profit-oriented firms cannot meet human needs; massive, centralized, bureaucratized hospitals stifle the exploration for new techniques and remove medical care from the communities where people live.

For the Greens, a system which gives priority to economic goals over ecological, social and democratic considerations will end up paying countless hidden costs; a short-sighted preoccupation with technology, profit and bureaucracy will be less economical in the long run than an approach which takes these other dimensions fully into account from the start.

But the Greens are more concerned that the same faulty set of priorities has led to massive environmental and social damage. Deforestation, toxic waste, endangered species, acid rain, water pollution, unhealthy food, ozone depletion, excessive noise, poaching, vivisection, and radiation—all allegedly result from a system dominated by technology, profit, bureaucracy, and the "throw-away" mentality.

There is also a human cost in mounting feelings of powerlessness and alienation. Petra Kelly declares, "We are all becoming replaceable and the replaceability of the individual is a new social experience of death."[13] Modern Germany is said to discriminate against women in the marketplace, in education and in social welfare, by providing inadequate remuneration for childraising, brief (six-month) maternity leaves, and inadequate birth control facilities. Older people and children are powerless, left in the wake of modern society's progress. There is exploitation of foreign guest workers, ill treatment of gypsies, and discrimination in housing, employment, adoption, child care, psychiatry, and against homosexuals.

The Greens contend that consumer society engenders a type of scientific inquiry that serves commercial ends at the expense of human needs, and that a centralized, rigidly bureaucratized educational system represses innovation and initiative by students, parents and teachers, while ignoring the cultivation of values, creativity and ecological "consciousness." Another

---

[13]Kelly, "Das System ist bankrott," *op. cit.*, p. 136.

cost of modern society is the growth of a culture which the Greens say is qualitatively and physically remote from the everyday life of people because it lies in the hands of "culture industries" or bureaucracies and is controlled by a few participants. Private interests reputedly also dominate the mass media, especially newspapers, closing out "real alternative views" and thus constricting freedom of opinion.

A concentration of power is also blamed for what the Greens see as an increasingly "authoritarian" political system. Because entrenched elites want to preserve their position, they limit citizen participation to occasional elections which effectively offer only a choice between two evils—candidates nominated by two closed, centralized, oligarchical parties. The Establishment also preserves its grip through the requirement that parties must earn 5 percent of the vote to receive legislative seats, and through the ban on radicals holding public jobs, censorship of the press, restricted use of referenda and citizens' initiatives, and exploitation of computerized data about personal matters. This alleged power monopoly forces dissent into the streets where, it is charged, order is maintained by use of limitations on public assembly, tear gas, mass internment (in Bavaria), and riot police.

## Evaluating the Criticisms

Clear contradictions exist within the Greens' censure of Germany's economic and political institutions and dire predictions for the future of German society—contradictions that can often be traced back to the movement's heterogeneous composition. The most obvious contending streams of thought within the movement divide over the question of whether environmental conditions or unemployment should be the primary focus of concern. Rudolf Bahro, a leading Green ideologist, puts so much emphasis on ecological themes that he is even willing to let the German economy "collapse under the weight of five million unemployed,"[14] while like-minded "fundamentalist" Greens argue that unemployment can even help to hasten revolutionary change and suggest that too much concern about paychecks is "bourgeois." More pragmatic "reformers" respond that unemployment must be the first concern of a truly "social" movement.

There are other contradictions. The Greens' overall program condemns, in sweeping terms, the technological impulse of modern scientific-industrial society. While stopping short of Luddite extremes, they make clear their contempt for technology in general because it destroys the environment and "controls men." Thus, the movement inevitably denounces the

---

[14]*Der Spiegel*, November 22, 1982, p. 31.

technological dynamic which also produces innovations they approve of, those which are ecologically safe and "social," from lightweight metals and Germany's rail system to solar cells, higher mileage cars and recycling processes. To be sure, movement spokesmen struggle to draw self-serving distinctions between "good" and "bad" technology, but their program in effect "throws out the baby with the bath water."

There is a clear stream of elitism in the movement's critique as well. On the basis of their proclaimed ascetic and humanitarian standards, the Greens scornfully dismiss the values of bourgeois society as shallow and crassly materialistic, claiming they are created by corporate manipulation of consumer demand. White- and blue-collar German citizens are given little credit for being able to form their own values, and even those things they appear to choose freely are condemned by the Greens. For example, the movement declares, "We are of the opinion that the normal citizen has no need for these technical innovations (like cable television)," and that under pressure to finance cable television, broadcasters will present "insipid" programming.[15] Yet, these programs would probably be profitable precisely because many Germans would choose to watch them. Also, in the disregard many Greens show for trade union wage concerns, there is evidence of what one Social Democrat characterized as "elitist-bourgeois" attitudes.[16]

Green rhetoric crosses the line between polemical extremism and outright scare-mongering. For the Greens, all of today's problems are not merely grave, but "scandalous," "disastrous," *Lebensgefährlich*—threats to life itself. "Poisonous," "destructive," "dangerous," "exploitative," "devastating," "repressive," "authoritarian," and "totalitarian," are words used by Greens to describe the society around them. Their opponents earn colorful titles like *Totengräbers* (gravediggers—a term used to describe irresponsible conservatives who undermined Weimar Germany and helped bring Hitler to power), or are simply denounced as corrupt, authoritarian and oligarchical. This *Angst,* or anxiety, is out of proportion to what average Germans and a large number of German youths feel, whatever their view of technology and industrialization. Even those who are sympathetic to the Greens note that "most Germans find that things go well for them," and analysts point out that opinion poll data corroborate this observation.[17]

---

[15] *Bay* (Medien).

[16] Klaus Matthiesen, in *Die Neue Gesellschaft,* IX 1980, cited in Rudolf Scharping and Joachim Hofmann-Göttig, "'Alternative' Politik in den Landesparlamenten? Ideologiekritische Inhaltsanalyse von 300 Redebeiträgen 'grüner' Parlametarier," *Zeitschrift für Parlamentsfragen,* Vol. 3, Fall 1982, p. 401.

[17] Erhard Eppler, *Wege aus der Gefahr* (Hamburg: Rowohlt Verlag, 1981), p. 136.

In this tendency to exaggerate the bleakness of their lives, there is a certain strain of paranoia, or at the very least a strong sense of victimization at the hands of others. Petra Kelly declares that the "greatest disclosure story of our time would be [one that] uncovers the dark connections of military budgets and state debts, energy crises and inflation and multinational concerns." The omnipotent villains of this plot are not named, although she implicates the Trilateral Commission and the Reagan Administration.[18] There are other examples. Although West Germany is a world leader in technical research, the Greens deplore the conniving "private economic interests" behind it. While Germany has a thriving press—which has helped propel the Greens to public prominence—and countless "alternative" newspapers and magazines, the Greens decry private interests which allegedly control the media and threaten free expression.

Nowhere is this creeping paranoia that impels the Green program more evident than in attitudes toward government policies on civil rights. In the early 1980s, only one demonstrator has been killed (accidentally) by authorities, despite numerous clashes between police and protestors, generally instigated by the latter; only one questionable mass internment has been undertaken (by Bavarian authorities against demonstrators protesting housing shortages in Nuremberg); and prison conditions even for terrorists meet international human rights standards. Yet the Greens claim that these circumstances reflect "an unlimited application of the official power monopoly," a "nearly military struggle against citizens," and the growth of "strong tendencies toward authoritarian measures and a 'big brother' state"; Petra Kelly even sees creeping totalitarianism in the "atomic state."[19] Although there were countless large-scale protests between 1980 and 1983, the Greens deplore "massive limits on the freedom to assemble." They see computer technology as a chilling threat because personal data could be recorded by the authorities and used against private citizens. On these grounds, the Greens blocked so routine a measure as the planned 1983 census.

Not only do these exaggerated suspicions of the West German state suggest a strong sense of victimization but, given the Federal Republic's successful record in all these areas—health care, research, media freedom, civil liberties—the Green criticisms are inaccurate and unjustified as well. They virulently condemn the environmental destruction wrought by "economic growth that is oriented only toward profit," but do not

---

[18]Petra Kelly, "Wie sich die Ökologiebewegung Zum Friedensbewegung erweiterte, Variante A," in Kelly and Leinen, editors, *op. cit.*, p. 11.

[19]*Ibid.*, p. 13.

mention that the Federal Republic's most polluted major river—the Elbe—carries an enormous amount of waste from East Germany, or that the area of West Germany worst hit by acid rain receives the fallout of uncontrolled brown-coal-burning power stations and factories in neighboring Czechoslovakia.[20]. There is also some question about the honesty of an environmental program that condemns current production methods for their high cost when, in many cases, these expenses resulted from steps taken to reduce ecological damage. Sometimes the Greens are caught up in their own exaggerated and unfair accusations. They hint darkly that there is an Establishment conspiracy to protect former "co-conspirators and backers of fascism," who have "occupied key political and economic positions," yet one ex-Nazi storm trooper who did indeed make a successful career in the 1980s was Werner Vogel, nominated as honorary 1983 Bundestag speaker by his party—the Greens themselves.[21]

## Green Alternatives for Germany

When it comes to economic structure, the Greens espouse "a complete revolution of our short-term oriented economic *Zweckdenkens* (thought goals)."[22] Economic recovery, in the Greens' view, can be achieved only by a more enlightened overall approach, involving energy conservation, recyclable materials, more durable goods, as well as "a ban on all substances and processes that destroy the ecological balance."[23] Green leader Rainer Trampert cites the OECD's conclusion that environmental damage costs Germany 50 to 70 billion marks annually, and he implies that a Green program could recoup those losses.[24] Such ecological measures would be complemented by various steps, including the thorough evaluation of technology for its environmental impact, "objective consumer information" provided independent of private corporations, an immediate ban on advertising for environmentally unsound products, and new patent laws to assure safer goods. While these measures reflect the desires of "fundamentalist" Greens who stress ecological improvements, the "reformists" advocate more Marxist-oriented steps, which, despite some controversy, appear in Green programs. Thus, the conditions of labor, claim the Greens, must also be improved before economic health can be restored, and the necessary measures should include a guaranteed secure income for all; a "just division of labor"; an unlimited right

---

[20]*Bay* (Präambel, Ökologisch); *Financial Times,* April 14, 1983, p. 2.
[21]*Bay* (Demokratie), p. 35.
[22]*BP* (Präambel, Einleitung), p. 4.
[23]*Ibid.* (Grundlagen und Ziele grüner Wirtschaftspolitik), p. 7.
[24]*Die Zeit,* March 4, 1983, p. 3.

to strike; reduction of the work week to 35 hours, with wage equalization and wage increases (a proposal contested by the ecological fundamentalists); reduction of the work span through longer periods of education and flexible retirement ages; reduction of the work year through longer vacations, including "educational vacations"; the elimination of overtime; and a ban on pay cuts.

All of these measures will take place, the Greens say, in an economic system administered at the local level by planners mindful of "regional-specific mixed economies"; in a more democratic workplace in which labor determines its own conditions of employment; and through unions administered entirely from the "basis." Nationalization is rejected because it leads to a situation where economic life is not controlled by the "basis."[25] The tools by which this restructuring of the economy will occur include "investment that takes social duties into account"; greater opportunities for job training; the removal of unnecessary regulations and the establishment of new rules, such as those concerning noise, safety and health in the workplace, and labor rights; the lifting of income taxes from those with low incomes; and institution of graduated taxes on luxury goods.

To all these changes, there is a unifying theme: If the overall natural, social and political environment is substantially improved and becomes more liveable, economic problems will take care of themselves. While "reformers" emphasize short-term, worker-oriented measures, "fundamentalists" are even more willing to espouse waiting for long-term structural changes to take effect—even at the expense of some "belt-tightening" in the present.[26]

This same basic assumption underlies the Greens' alternative solutions for specific sectors of the overall socioeconomic system. Energy plays a particularly central role in the movement's vision of a more liveable future; they believe that conservation and certain alternative sources of energy are economical, but also claim that their approach will prove more secure, safe and clean. In this area the Greens advance a host of theories and models developed by experts who espouse "the soft-path"—regenerative, passive, nonfossil fuel sources of power generation. The movement would ban the construction of nuclear power plants, eliminate existing ones, and phase out fossil fuels, above all oil, although coal might, under certain circumstances, be used. Whatever share of demand these sources currently cover need not be entirely replaced, the Greens claim, because present consumption patterns are artificially high. Conservation thus "is

---

[25]*Die Zeit*, January 28, 1983, p. 4.
[26]*Ibid.*

seen as the most important energy source, "because reduced, realistic demand can lower the overall use of energy. For the movement, conservation should include better "technical" use of power: construction of homes to maximize solar heating (larger windows facing south, for example); widespread use of insulation in homes and businesses; an emphasis on mass transit and a reduction of overall transport; and the establishment of speed limits on the *Autobahnen*. Such measures could, according to the claims of the Bavarian Green Party, cut German energy use in half. Additional "structural" conservation could further reduce demand: the production of longer-lasting goods; high-mileage automobiles; decentralized production to decrease energy-intensive transport; a tax on raw material consumption; the expanded use of trains and street cars in place of cars, trucks and jet planes. Overall, the Green conservation philosophy is said to be geared primarily toward "meeting needs," not providing energy.

Whatever energy *is* needed could, according to the Greens, be supplied by a host of alternative means: reprocessed heat application, solar heating, heat pumps, biogas and wind. Architectural designs could be reworked to maximize the use of these sources, especially solar heat and solar current, while meat consumption could be reduced to free grain for biomass. (Certain other alternatives, like coal liquefaction, to say nothing of nuclear fusion, are discarded.) In short, the Greens assert that even the current level of economic growth could, if necessary, be maintained by using alternative energy sources, while a "people-oriented" Green economy, with widespread conservation and far less demand for growth, could easily be sustained by the "soft path" approach to energy.

The Greens' vision of the future includes reducing private means of transportation to a minimum, giving priority instead to the funding and construction of local mass transit, trains and bicycles. Automobiles and buses with much greater mileage capabilities and lower emissions would be designed and produced. Speed limits and urban traffic-free zones would be encouraged, and large-scale jet airports discouraged.

Housing needs in a Green Germany, it is claimed, would be met by enacting laws to renovate older buildings rather than building large modern apartment complexes, and to create parks to make urban residential areas more liveable. At the same time, decentralized economic structures would help spread the population into outlying areas and alleviate pressure on city housing. Buying up empty housing for the purpose of real estate speculation would be forbidden, and laws favorable to tenants strengthened.

Regarding rural life and work, the Greens advocate an end to farming methods dependent on fossil fuels and chemicals, and a gradual shift to "ecologically oriented" agriculture for "healthier," more natural foods. This would entail testing organic substances and processes (including mixed planting to replace monocultures), using organic fertilizers, and educating farmers in the new approach. To replace agri-business and agri-bureaucracy, the Greens plan to end farm subsidies, ship surpluses to developing countries, institute direct marketing of produce, and put decisionmaking power in the hands of local farm groups.

Most of the Green environmental program is implicit in the movement's vision of the economy as a whole, but there are specific measures for the planning, monitoring and enforcing of the above changes to ensure that all ecological goals are met. There would be no exemptions from such regulations, and persons or organizations responsible for violations would have to bear the cost of reparations. The Greens argue that health criteria must always supersede financial ones.[27] Thus, they propose an environmental protection policy that will ban the use of asphalt in many areas, fluoride in drinking water, asbestos in buildings, phosphates in detergents, all toxic substances, and eventually even gasoline (once methanol is widely produced). There would also be comprehensive tests for and bans on all potential carcinogens, materials which deplete the ozone layer, and unnecessarily noisy engines, again without regard to financial considerations. The landscape would be preserved by strict zoning laws banning, among other things, superhighways and large-scale canals and airports, as well as ski-lifts and major sports complexes. The Greens also claim that they will eradicate poaching, "reorganize" hunting and fishing along ecological lines, and reduce medical experimentation on animals—"Tests on live animals may not be more painful than would be tolerable in operations on humans."[28]

Part of a Green Germany, as outlined by the movement's programs, would be reform in the area of equal rights for women. The Greens propose abolishing all categories which make distinctions on the basis of sex in education and employment, recognizing housewives' work for the purpose of paying pensions, exempting women from the armed services, constructing new women's centers, providing female judges for court cases involving women, and expanding the legal definition of sex crimes to include more than rape alone. The Greens also advocate compensating parents who take time off to educate children or to care for sick children, while expanding paid maternity leaves to eighteen months and providing

---

[27]*BP* (Umwelt und Gesundheit), p. 45.
[28]*Bay* (Natur und Umwelt).

free abortions and birth control. The two latter elements of their program would be removed from the purview of the judiciary.

The movement proposes equal rights for minorities as well, along with bilingual education and immediate voting rights in local elections for guest workers; compensation to gypsies for their treatment under Hitler, a ban on any attempt to settle them, and official support for their culture; and finally, for homosexuals, compensation for victims of the Nazis, a complete end to discrimination in pensions, employment, retirement, justice, adoption, and child care programs, and a constitutional amendment assuring equal rights.

Education, culture and the mass media would be "democratized," which, according to the Green definition, means restructured schools (smaller classes, greater opportunities for "alternative," that is private, nonparochial, education), more vocational training, more "experiential" learning, more education in "ecological" matters, and even more political involvement for students. Academic research would be removed from the hands of private commercial interests and structured more "democratically," with oversight commissions to monitor the ecological implications of scientific industry. Consumerism's alleged grip on culture and mass media must also be eased, say the Greens. They propose extended public support for decentralized, local, alternative and minority influence in art, theater groups and newspapers, discouragement of "consumer"-oriented television and cable television, and the tight limitation of privately-owned printed media.

The Greens' desire to end what they see as the concentration of total power in the Establishment's hands emerges most clearly in their program for reforming civil and political rights. Decentralized public administration will, they claim, assure a more social, "basis democratic" and nonviolent public administration. In addition, they advocate eliminating the 5 percent minimum vote for parliamentary representation, using plebiscites and citizens initiatives more often, permitting civil disobedience, opening up political parties to "basis" control, and imposing limits on a politician's time in office. The Greens would remove all current limits on demonstrations, rescind the law barring radicals from public employment, and prevent the police from carrying guns, using tear gas, conducting house searches and opening mail without a warrant. In penal law they advocate vastly expanded rehabilitation facilities in and out of prison.

### Evaluating the Alternatives

"They ask interesting questions. But they don't give interesting answers."[29] Social Democrat Egon Bahr made this observation about the Greens, but

---

[29]Markham, *op. cit.*

it characterizes the reaction of many observers familiar with the Greens. While many Germans sympathize with the movement and its concerns, particularly environmental problems, the Greens' program of alternative policies is taken far less seriously.

What critics find most frustrating in the Green approach to public policy formulation is that the movement seems to offer either no alternative proposals of its own or wildly implausible ones that lack concreteness. It frequently appears that Greens prefer to remain "nay-sayers" or to flaunt their idealism rather than advance anything that might carry the risk of having to cooperate with the established parties. Petra Kelly and almost all major Green leaders (with rare exceptions, such as Baden-Württemberg's Wolf-Dieter Hasenclever) stress that the party must never compromise on questions of the environment, democracy, equal rights and the economy. Hamburg's Thomas Ebermann agreed that "The ability to compromise is not one of our goals."[30] One SPD analyst quotes the words of a Green representative in Berlin to reinforce the point that the Greens concentrate primarily on forming a profile "that consists of opposing the parties [which back] the dynamic of industrialism."[31] The negativism of the Green approach to forming new domestic policies is characterized by one of the movement's delegates who resisted a particular piece of reform by declaring, "I don't have any patent remedies to offer here, but we want to prevent you from making unconscionable immoral decisions."[32]

When the Greens do advance alternatives such as those summarized in the previous section, they are often contradictory, vague or unrealistic. One major reason for this is the movement's heterogeneity. As SPD critics observed, "while until now they have been united mostly through 'nay-saying,' [they] are divided by the [need to formulate] concrete alternatives."[33] This is true, above all, in the area of socioeconomic transformation. Within the movement's program and among its many statements, there is talk about how to sustain growth, provide jobs, and satisfy the trade unions (with shorter workweeks for example), yet significant Green spokesmen declare that "we are not here to defend or create jobs . . . it is not our goal to bring 'bread and wages' to everyone again . . . . there is not too little but too much work."[34] These and other conflicts in approach

---

[30]*Der Spiegel*, September 20, 1982, p. 40.
[31]Scharping and Hofmann-Göttig, *op. cit.*, p. 397.
[32]*Ibid.*
[33]*Die Grünen A3*, SPD pamphlet, 1983.
[34]Rudolf Bahro, "Grüne Grundposition," Working Paper for the Hagen Party-day, p. 2, cited in *Die Rotgrünen Argumente gegen die rotgrünen Experimente* (Bonn: CDU-Bundesgeschaftstelle, 1983), p. 12.

reflect the movement's internal divisions among various *Länder* parties, such as Berlin's urban Alternatives and Baden-Württemberg's rural Greens; Marxists and non-Marxists; "reformists" and "fundamentalists"; and various interest groups, such as students, feminists, farmers, homosexuals, workers and others. Thus, while no party's political platform is ever a model of philosophical clarity, the Greens' various formal programs on the *Land* and federal levels are not only contradictory in many cases, but vague and ambiguous by design apparently to avoid alienating various factions.

The Greens are confident that they can improve all areas of socioeconomic life by following their leitmotifs and creating a new environment conducive to "qualitative growth"—expansion that "really matters" to people and is ecologically safe. Such optimism leads them to disregard practical problems about the feasibility of technical innovations they would promote, especially alternative energy sources, but also organic farming, decentralized production, alternative transport and other items. For proof that these concepts will work, the Greens turn to selected data from Establishment sources, "soft-path" scientists, and various academic models outlining "qualitative growth," but since no other country has been able to put most of these technologies to work, hard evidence of their utility and success is lacking. Thus, for example, Rainer Trampert can cite authoritative studies indicating that all the heat lost through factory smokestacks, if rechanneled, could generate twice the power presently generated by nuclear power, but he does not offer suggestions of how that would be undertaken or what it would cost.[35] Likewise, the energy platform of the Hessen Green Party claims that 80 percent of the country's demand for electricity could be covered by regenerative sources, but, as a CDU critic observed, "The fact that, according to the information of serious experts, [regenerative energy sources] in the foreseeable future could cover from 5 percent to at the most 10 percent of our energy needs, does not seem to seriously irritate the Greens in their wish world."[36]

Perhaps more importantly, political rivals and nonpartisan observers see in the Green approach a tendency to ignore economic relationships and interconnections. Critics point out that while the Greens claim that they can increase output by "humanizing" work conditions and reducing the workweek to 35 hours, the movement, once in power, would simultaneously undermine the position of large companies which account for half of Germany's production—and thus millions of those jobs. Social Democrats argue that in this and other respects, the Greens ignore orga-

---

[35]*Die Zeit*, March 4, 1983, p. 3.

[36]Erwin Teufel, "Die Grünen—Zwischen Bewegung und Partei," *Sonde*, Fall 1982, p. 6.

nized labor's role in the economy and demonstrate "a clear distance from trade union goals."[37] Moreover, there is doubt about how all of the party's proposed investments will be channeled. If there is neither profit nor planning, what will facilitate economic decisionmaking? Even a left-wing Berlin newspaper was moved to observe that Greens "leave open the question of who should invest and with what capital . . . . the Greens must explain which motive for investment would effectively replace the profit principle."[38]

Thus, while the Greens like to claim that they alone think about the long term, two SPD analysts examining the *Landtag* speeches of movement leaders concluded that "the social and societal effects of their finance proposals on other areas of policy are at least not mentioned."[39] Even nonpartisan critics are struck by the Greens' unwillingness to consider financial questions seriously. When party leader Rainer Trampert claimed that a cleaner environment would spare Germany billions of marks annually, a *Die Zeit* correspondent countered by observing, "The application of vigorous limits for the improvement or preservation of the environment would probably first have the effect of increasing costs in production." Trampert gave no clear reply.[40]

This disregard for financial relationships is all the more serious when the Greens try to explain how their program would be financed. Beyond asserting that a sweeping social transformation will pay for itself by reducing the long-term costs of the modern, industrial, bureaucratic system, the Greens limit themselves "to platitudinous proposals about the implementation and financing of their objectives [that] leave out of consideration the projected overall volume of finance."[41] In a modest reform program this would be serious enough, but few observers can put a price tag on the Green movement's package of changes which amounts to a comprehensive overhaul of each sector of West German society. Simple phrases such as "[we advocate] the construction of schools for the handicapped," or ideas like pensions for housewives, mandatory "low-cost personal transit," burying all electric cables, eighteen-month paid maternity leaves, reimbursement to parents who take time off from work to educate their children, and free therapy for drug addicts would be costly enough. Added to even more expensive programs, including longer vacations, shorter workweeks, and earlier retirement, to say nothing of

---

[37]Scharping and Hofmann-Göttig, *op. cit.*, p. 404.
[38]*Die Tagezeitung*, July 29, 1982, cited in *Die Rotgrünen, op. cit.*, p. 17.
[39]Scharping and Hofmann-Göttig, *op. cit.*, p. 398.
[40]*Die Zeit*, March 4, 1983, p. 3.
[41]Scharping and Hofmann-Göttig, *op. cit.*, p. 398.

vague but sweeping proposals for "decentralized production," "wage equalization," "new types of houses," "guaranteed incomes," and alternative energy sources, there is no question that the Green vision of the future would carry a gigantic price tag. Critics in the CDU/CSU estimate that just two of the myriad Green proposals—lowering the age limit for pensioners to 55, and full payment to widows (widowers) of their deceased husbands' (wives') pensions—would cost 50 billion marks (more than 20 billion dollars) per year. While approving the goals of many such programs, the CDU observed that the Greens foresee an "unlimited quantitative increase [in them] without considerations of the financial costs," while the SPD responds that "it is irresponsible to present many cost-intensive demands without saying something about financing (a catalog of goods without a list of prices is no alternative)."[42] There are signs that even the movement itself has doubts. A major working paper on economics delivered at the Green Party's Hagen conference conceded "for financing [these policies] the money is lacking."[43]

Moreover, the Greens claim they would try to undertake all of these programs while simultaneously reducing revenue through comprehensive tax cuts and incentives for "ecologically-oriented" innovations and gradually eliminating all taxes on those with "lower incomes." What is more, inflation, investment and business confidence are assumed to be stable external factors, even in the face of sweeping socioeconomic change. For a movement prone to ridicule American neoconservatives and "supply-side" theorists, the Greens could be more accurately accused of promoting "voodoo economics."

They also assert that their economic—and social—programs could be administered at the lowest regional or local level and by private communal associations, or "small networks." As conceived by the Greens, the feasibility of this concept is questioned even by conservatives who have long opposed over-centralization; Social Democrats fear the Green program would end up destroying the "social welfare state" altogether.[44]

This tendency of the Greens to "limit themselves to formulating goals and disregarding the questions of political implementation"[45] plagues the movement's alternatives for administration as well as policy. The movement demands that the people directly concerned (*die Betroffenen*) should

---

[42]*Die Grünen A3*, SPD pamphlet, 1983.
[43]"Wirtschaftspapier" of the Greens at the Hagen Party-day, cited in *Die Rotgrünen, op. cit.*, p. 11.
[44]Scharping and Hofmann-Göttig, *op. cit.*, p. 401.
[45]*Die Grünen A3*, SPD pamphlet, 1983.

have a direct input in determining all policy—"basis" democracy—and, thus, it advocates national and local plebiscites, along with various citizen oversight commissions in academic research groups, all political parties, and all levels of government. Nowhere is it explicitly stated what constitutes "the concerned": in cases such as the construction of a nuclear plant, would they be those people living directly in the vicinity, those employed by the project, those receiving the power, or all of these groups? Two SPD critics noted that the Greens have not answered these questions and others, such as "How can complex matters be reduced to a 'yes/no' alternative?"; and concluded that the movement "appears hardly to have thought through the individual structural elements and clearly the consequences of 'basis democracy.'"[46]

A major Green goal, inherent in their four leitmotifs, is to end bureaucratization—yet, the movement's program for change actually points toward a massive expansion of governmental administration and regulation. With ample reason, the CDU charges that "where [the Greens] become concrete—as occasionally in social policy—their proposals lead to the opposite of what they themselves strive against, namely, to more bureaucratic centralism."[47] The examples are legion. Assuring compliance with proposed rules or tax changes on conservation in the home and office, manufacture of more durable goods, recycling, "objective" consumer testing, strengthened quality control, reduced truck travel, bans on a wide variety of chemicals and toxic substances, and new emissions standards, will require massive oversight. Vague ideas of "developing new technologies," redirecting investment to more "social" ends, more social and ecological town planning, "furthering" entirely new types of research in energy, farming, forestry, psychiatry, medicine (such as "natural means of healing") and other areas, as well as new and expanded forms of training, education and public information—all of this broad package strongly suggests a need for new regulations, agencies, planning, taxes, and thus inevitably, bureaucracy. Although the Greens specifically call for all of these changes to be implemented at the lowest possible level, they adduce no evidence that local bureaucracies would necessarily be less cumbersome, costly or intrusive than those in Bonn, especially since their duties would apparently involve more and entirely new areas of control. What is more, if the common standards they describe as critical are to be met, these changes would require some degree of federal oversight that might far exceed what presently exists, even though in new or different sectors and forms.

---

[46]Scharping and Hofmann-Göttig, *op. cit.*, p. 407.
[47]Die Rotgrünen, *op. cit.*, p. 25.

There is a final and perhaps most serious set of reasons why the Greens vision of Germany's future is flawed. While claiming that its aim, its very ethos, is to expand personal autonomy and the scope for individual self-determination, the movement outlines an idiosyncratic form of democracy that persuades, guides and occasionally even compels its citizens' choices in all areas of life. Movement ideologists apparently assume that their own post-industrial elitist "morally-grounded asceticism" and activism is shared or should be emulated by all Germans. By imposing their own standards on the marketplace, for example, the Greens would eliminate the flexibility and the substantial element of personal choice provided by consumer capitalism. This would be done not only through the aforementioned expansion of bureaucratic restrictions, but also by banning—and thus preventing people from having—a whole category of goods deemed "unecological": second homes, certain kinds of tourism, jet travel inside Germany, ski-lifts, cable television, and other new forms of communications technology. The Greens claim that demand for these and other goods has been artificially stimulated through promotion and even subsidies, and that people would otherwise not necessarily choose to buy or use them. Yet the Greens' program is susceptible to the same charge. For example, if the Green government encourages mass transit, while placing regulations and special taxes on automobile travel, the net effect would be to transform Germany's entire system of personal transport regardless of what consumers, left to their own devices, might prefer. There are equally troubling implications "for individual freedoms" in the Greens' willingness to "restructure property rights" in the name of cheap housing.[48] One need hardly defend crass materialism and greedy slumlords to ask whether the Greens' program places their own professed values ahead of free choice in the marketplace.

Equally disturbing for a society based on freedom of choice is the movement's program for "consciousness-raising" measures that amount to a comprehensive campaign of public education, or perhaps re-education, along the lines of its four leitmotifs. Green goals would be "encouraged," "furthered," or "strengthened," for example, by subjecting scientific research to oversight by commissions assessing the "long-term consequences for ecology," or requiring that public education stress the development of "ecological consciousness." Greens justify this "guidance" by claiming that private (commercial) interests have dominated research and education, and that the deleterious effects must now be ameliorated. Yet, their proposals again seem to stress their own political criteria much more than the need for open and objective inquiry.

---

[48]Uwe Moller, "Was will die Grun-Alternative Liste," *Rissener Rundbrief*, September 1982.

The same applies to Green plans for policy alternatives in the cultural field. While claiming that the expressive arts should be made "more democratic" and open than the current Establishment's "consumer culture" permits, the Greens then go on to list what culture "must" provide—elitist standards buried in egalitarian rhetoric, to be fostered by the use of public resources. Cultural institutions, for example, "must consider more than hitherto the needs and everyday problems of the population"; "alternative areas of culture" which stimulate thinking about cultural forms and content, and in which as many people as possible can participate are "to be strongly promoted"; the cultural budget must encourage the development of "'basis' [grass roots] culture."[49] Mass media must also meet Green standards: the movement would end today's alleged oligarchical control of the press by limiting private financial influence on the media and providing government support for (an already thriving) "alternative media" scene, while requiring that "minority interests" receive proper attention.

Paradoxically, there may also be troubling consequences for German parliamentary institutions in the Green movement's plan to make administrative and political life more "basis" democratic. Many Greens seem to believe that such a reform would restrict, perhaps even eliminate, parliamentarianism. All movement members consider representative government to be insufficiently "direct," and regard it as an irksome obstacle that they would ideally circumscribe or circumvent, while more extreme activists want it abolished. (Some Greens even express a desire to emulate Libyan Colonel Khaddafi's destruction of parliamentary rule.)[50]

Just as their weariness with representative government bespeaks a distaste for the give and take of pragmatic politics, the Greens' own preferred political concept, plebiscites, raises doubt about the democratic soundness of a Green political system. Numerous plebiscites, by their very aim of rewarding engagement in the process and punishing noninvolvement, may create a system dominated by activists and one too demanding for the average citizen. Those charged with phrasing public propositions, and determining which "concerned" citizens would be enfranchised in voting on local issues like power plant construction, would have as much power as present-day "oligarchical" politicians. Moreover, people willing and able to spend time becoming acquainted with countless specific issues—mainly the middle class, highly educated, active citizens, such as sympathizers of the Greens—would be favored by plebiscitary measures, while frequent referenda might frustrate and disenchant those "not

---

[49]*BP* (Kultur), p. 42.
[50]*New York Times*, July 27, 1982.

in the active minorities."⁵¹ Partly for these reasons, the German Basic Law rejects *Volksdemokratie*; for it should be remembered that, after a point, it was largely through plebiscites that the Nazis consolidated their rule without the need for parliamentary action. In short, the Greens want a politicized society. Their other reform measures—group rights, wider use of citizens' initiatives, strict limits on a politician's time in office—are all designed to reward the activist "basis," but may thus punish the average citizen who, by free choice, is a passive participant.

As current Green protest tactics and Green policy programs indicate, the movement's preference for nonparliamentary political activity is a disturbing, self-serving definition of legality. Their emphasis on "nonviolence" theoretically excludes violence against persons, but not violence against "objects" by private citizens "concerned" about their "life-sustaining interests." Individual Green leaders openly justify violence for political goals—"The court of final judgment about the extent, form and intensity of civil opposition is the 'conscience of the individual' or of 'the group.'" This leads critics to charge that the Greens fail to recognize "that in our free constitutional state there is only a right to resist totalitarian grabs for power, but not to achieve one's political goals through violence."⁵² They add that, when the Greens classify rent speculation as illegal, but expand the concept of legal action to justify those actions they sympathize with, including the occupation of empty houses, they "relativize the civil-liberty state."⁵³

## The Green View of International Affairs

### Green Criticisms of the West's Foreign Policy

The Greens charge that the unecological, antisocial and undemocratic way of thinking and the obsession with force which they claim dominate modern German society also characterize the conduct of global affairs by the industrialized world—above all the West. This mentality is said to result in policies that sustain confrontation between the blocs, particularly the rivalry of a deadly nuclear arms race, while perpetuating and exploiting the Third World's underdevelopment—circumstances which give rise to repression, conflict and impending Armageddon.

The Greens see the East-West rivalry as the primary "dynamic of self-destruction." Unlike other Germans, they claim bloc confrontation entails neither a fundamental conflict of principles and systems nor a largely

---

⁵¹Scharping and Hofmann-Göttig, *op. cit.*, p. 407.
⁵²*Die Rotgrünen, op. cit.*, p. 24.
⁵³*Ibid.*

one-sided threat of expansion from the Soviet Union. In the movement's perspective, there are few intrinsic differences between the industrialized systems of Western-style liberalism and Soviet-style socialism. They note the absence of "human rights" in the East but dismiss any notion that the West is defending real democracy. They see only "graduated" differences between conditions in the two blocs. The Greens view Moscow's motives as primarily defensive, if crudely assertive and "accident-prone." Thus, they declare "it is untrue that we are threatened by an unprovoked attack from the East."[54]

What really accounts for the intensity—and danger—of East-West competition in the Green view is not Soviet repression or expansion, but a *mutual,* self-perpetuating battle for hegemony between the elite ruling circles of both superpowers who "wage their daily rivalry on the backs of the peoples."[55] Moscow and Washington are engaged in a power struggle, dividing the world into spheres of interest and influence. It is the logic of this bloc power rivalry, not the nature of the Kremlin's system or policies, that accounts for repression in the East and the West as well as Soviet expansion. Human rights are said to be violated in Eastern Europe and the Soviet Union because, under the pressure of militarization, the communist regime has adopted reactionary, repressive measures. As for Soviet expansion, "an actual threat to Western Europe from the Soviet Union exists only insofar as the Soviet Union itself sees a threatening military potential [in the West]."[56]

In fact, the Greens argue that the United States, by pursuing the deadly global power struggle through direct intervention, arms exports and military training, has put the Soviet Union on the defensive; thus, today "the peace is currently threatened above all by the expansionist policy of the USA."[57] Detente, as practiced by Washington and Bonn, offered some promise of change; but, because U.S. and German policymakers alike accepted the bloc division as permanent, they lost the opportunity to create real peace. The Greens charge that the U.S. leadership has long justified its policy in the power struggle by creating an ideological veneer comprised of anticommunist *Feindbilder*—fabricated depictions of the Eastern bloc as an intrinsically dangerous, aggressive totalitarian foe.

It follows from the movement's analysis that Europe, and above all Germany, are victimized by the East-West rivalry, and are not parties to it,

---

[54]Rudolf Bahro, "The SPD and the Peace Movement," *New Left Review,* January-February 1982, p. 121.

[55]Rudolf Bahro, *Socialism and Survival* (London: Heretic Books, 1982), p. 54.

[56]*Ham* (Frieden).

[57]*Ibid.*

let alone beneficiaries of it. The two superpowers hold a condominium over Europe at the expense of the Europeans. Thus, the Greens identify themselves with groups like Solidarity in Poland or Charter 77 in Czechoslovakia because all are fighting "bloc confrontation."

The Greens argue that Germany is particularly victimized by East-West rivalry. "Inclusion in the blocs," "the presence of foreign occupation" troops, Bonn's subordination to NATO's command structure—these circumstances have deprived Germany of "sovereignty." Worse yet, bloc division and its need for fabricated *Feindbilder* on both sides, but especially on the part of America and its CDU/CSU "proxies," have created a climate of mutual suspicion which "blocks political and social changes in the Federal Republic as well as in the GDR."[58] This division of Germany allows the superpowers to confront each other face-to-face in Central Europe, which thus becomes the likely battleground of a major conflagration. By subordinating the German problem to other policy goals, such as Western integration or superpower rapprochement, the CDU/CSU and SPD have cemented the country's division, failing to resolve Germany's division and damaging the interests of peace.

Bloc competition is blamed also for generating pressure to build more and more nuclear weapons, those technological demons that the Greens say reflect the flawed mentality of modern industrial society. In accordance with the dynamics of the arms race, each superpower must strive for superiority over the other, and they both demonstrate "the intention and readiness to use atomic weapons in carrying out their national interests." But primary blame is again placed on the United States: A Green-sponsored "Nuremberg Trial" convicted the United States of waging atomic war in 1945, initiating each new stage in the arms race, and continuing to "prepare and implement the massive use of atomic weapons."[59] This, it is charged, has strengthened the hand of Moscow's military-industrial complex, giving it an argument for its armaments buildup.

Today, the arms race is accelerating because, in order to keep ahead of the Soviets, America is relying on "the dissemination of untruths" about Soviet nuclear superiority, while claiming to discover "new gaps" in the Pentagon's arsenal so as to justify U.S. demands for more missiles. All this is done, the Greens charge, in the name of sustaining an arms "balance" which no one can define and a "deterrence" concept which is fictional—"an ineffective threat because it encompasses atomic self-destruction."[60]

---

[58]*Pakt*, p. 7.
[59]*Frankfurter Allgemeine Zeitung,* February 24, 1983, p. 5.
[60]*BP* (Europäische Friedenspolitik), p. 19.

Europe is seen as the victim not only of bloc rivalry but also of the arms race that this power struggle has spawned, because nowhere are these weapons more densely deployed than in Central Europe—i.e., Germany. The quantities and capabilities of these weapons are repeatedly stressed by the Greens to illustrate their destructive potential and their implications for Germany. But what gives their concerns such urgency is the superpower—again, especially American—strategy of confronting its "power political rival" with the threat of a limited nuclear war in Europe, with that continent's destruction "taken approvingly into consideration."[61]

American plans to deploy neutron weapons are cited as a prime example of the danger to Central Europe, but not surprisingly the Greens focus on theater nuclear forces, the issue that helped give rise to a successful peace movement. They acknowledge that Soviet SS-20 missiles endanger Europe, but as retired General Gert Bastian, now a Green member, declared, "the SS-20 stationing in no way opens such fundamentally new possibilities for nuclear war fighting" as the modernized weapons called for by NATO.[62] The Greens declare that, given the accuracy of the American Pershing and cruise missiles, their targets (Soviet military installations), their vulnerable basing modes, and the reduced "warning time" for Moscow resulting from their forward basing and short flight time (in the Pershing's case), the INF systems are "uniquely and alone first-strike weapons." The danger lies in the fact that as "first-strike systems"—a Cuban missile crisis in reverse—they will not only accelerate the arms race but even invite Soviet preemption ("in case of war these land-based systems would be a favored target of Soviet attack") or in some other manner lead to a nuclear conflict limited to Europe, and "will make of Western Europe a nuclear wasteland."[63] The Greens claim that their suspicions of U.S. intentions in this regard are confirmed by the allegedly lackadaisical American approach to arms reduction. Moreover, the U.S. insistence on modernizing NATO's INF forces shows that Germany is an American pawn. Rainer Trampert explained that the missiles indicate "we do not currently have any right of self-determination. What exists is the right of determination by the United States."[64]

It is the increasingly intricate relationship between "East-West" and "North-South" that, according to the Greens, makes today's situation particularly hazardous. Their line of reasoning blends "Club of Rome" warnings about limited resources with a Marxist-Leninist analysis of imperialism and the

---

[61] *FM*, p. 6.
[62] *Der Spiegel*, July 13, 1981, p. 40.
[63] *FM*, p. 6.
[64] *Die Zeit*, March 4, 1983, p. 3.

Brandt Commission's reports about aid. The Greens charge that to preserve control over world markets, the industrialized West has attempted to keep the Third World countries in a condition of dependence by transferring the Western life-style and the dynamic growth precepts—and thus large-scale, highly technical, overly concentrated development—to the poorer countries. These lands thus suffer deforestation, pollution, resource depletion, and all the ecological damage richer countries have experienced, but for the less developed countries the effects of a growth orientation are even more dangerous because their own weak economic structures are further crippled and distorted in the process. The Greens assert that present aid programs are insufficient and compound the problem of dependence by favoring large-scale, capital-intensive development projects.

Because perpetual poverty breeds discontent and protest, Western governments must back "inhumane" regimes willing to maintain firm political control and protect their economic interests. Since "it is in the logic of the bloc confrontation" that Moscow must also obtain clients in the Third World to keep up with the West, the superpower rivalry has been superimposed on underdeveloped regions of the globe. Given the number of possible conflict areas involving U.S. and Soviet interests, "any local conflict in any region of the world can set in operation the escalation of deterrence to the use of nuclear weapons."[65]

## Evaluating the Criticisms

In attempting to make international affairs fit the mold set by their own visceral, instinctive contempt for modern industrial society as epitomized by West Germany and the United States, the Greens have produced a distorted and unconvincing diagnosis of the world's manifold ills—a diagnosis which disregards the imperiled position of Western liberal values that they themselves take for granted.

By declaring that each bloc, meaning primarily each superpower, is largely impelled by the modern techno-industrial system's alleged appetite for power and wealth, and thus holding both camps mutually responsible for world tension, the Green analysis discounts or ignores altogether a major dynamic of East-West confrontation—the Soviet system, which in Vladimir Bukovsky's words, generates the need for both repression and expansion to avoid the risk of change:

The two sides of the Soviet regime—internal oppression and external aggression—are inseparably interlocked, creating a sort of vicious circle. The more the

---

[65]*FM*, p. 8.

regime becomes rotten inside, the more pains are taken by its leaders to present a formidable facade to the outside world. They need international tension as a thief needs the darkness of the night.[66]

The Greens argue that Moscow arms and expands out of defensive motives, but in reality the Kremlin's compelling concern is not to preserve its empire from military penetration by the rival bloc; the Soviet Union requires an assertive world policy at the expense of others' freedom—a fact the Greens ignore—in order to preserve its system, to compensate for its failure to provide basic liberties, prosperity, even equality. Contrary to the Greens' claim, the Soviets are not aggressive "only in so far as Soviets themselves are faced by a threatening military potential"; rather, the Kremlin is expansionist by necessity, and this aggressiveness is responsible, in large measure, for bloc confrontation. It is not primarily Western arms that Moscow fears, but the threat to the Kremlin's internal control posed by a different political system. As Bukovsky points out, the Soviets

cannot tolerate a democratic state close to their borders (and then, close to the borders of their buffer-states), because a bad example of thriving democracy so close at hand might prove to be too provocative.[67]

So determined are the Greens to exonerate the Soviet regime from primary responsibility for East-West tension that they dismiss many critical systemic differences as meaningless. They declare that the West's negative images *(Feindbilder)* of the Kremlin are distortions and fabrications comparable to Nazi Germany's propaganda against Jews—an incredible but unintentionally ironic analogy. Those *Feindbilder* supposedly even "frighten" Moscow into responding aggressively, a notion which prompted Bukovsky to observe wryly: "[W]e ought to be imposing strict self-censorship on anti-Soviet speeches lest we be faced with Soviet occupation of the entire world."[68]

Loathe to concede that bloc conflict is driven in large part by the Soviet system's intrinsic fear of democracy as represented by a Western society they themselves hate, the Greens instead struggle to equalize blame for the East-West rivalry by making absurd statements that only serve to invalidate their central thesis. Thus, past events like the Berlin Blockade and the erection of the Berlin Wall are explained not as initiatives taken by Moscow, but merely as unfortunate episodes related to Germany's "inclusion in the blocs." Berlin's "Wall, gun towers, automatic firing devices

---

[66]Vladimir Bukovsky, "The Soviet Role in the Peace Movement," in Ernest Lefever and E. Stephen Hunt, editors, *The Apocalyptic Premise: Nuclear Arms Debated* (Washington, D.C.: The Ethics & Public Policy Center, 1982), p. 199.

[67]*Ibid.*, p. 201.

[68]*Ibid.*, p. 180.

and minefields" are a matter of "disputed apportionment of guilt."[69] Though it was the NATO allies which requested INF modernization, the Greens claim the arms race in Europe stems from an effort by both superpowers "to apply military pressure on their own spheres of influence and political pressure on the other and on its alliance partners."[70] The Greens express fear "in the same measure" of missiles aimed at them and missiles designed to defend them. They try to offset 100,000 Soviet occupation troops in Afghanistan with the disputed American role in Chile's military putsch a decade ago, U.S. "threats" to intervene in the Persian Gulf "to keep oil prices low," and several dozen Pentagon advisors in El Salvador.

Since bloc rivalry, and no real systemic factors, account for repression, both superpowers are said to "repress" or "choke off" dissent; differences in the scale of this "repression" are not considered important. Any real distinctions between the systems—even the rather obvious one that the Soviet system would not tolerate a Green movement—are dismissed as inconsequential to bloc competition, and perceptions of such differences are attributed to *Feindbilder:* both systems "prepare" their societies for "warlike confrontation," caricaturizing the opponent as an "untameable animal" so that "crossing the threshold to the extermination of the enemy costs nothing."[71] This formula is applied equally to the Soviet bloc, with its perpetual propaganda machine, and to the West, where the free press and contending politicians assure diverse, sometimes sympathetic, views of Soviet policy.

In this painstaking effort to appear evenhanded and thus maintain the consistency of their perspective, the Greens treat the Soviet occupation of a dozen countries as an accident. Rudolf Bahro declares, for instance, that the Soviets made great sacrifices to "liberate" Czechoslovakia from Hitlerite Germany, and thus its 1968 intervention was understandable. At any rate, he believes the Soviets are in Eastern Europe against their will, fearful to withdraw because the United States might fill the vacuum; since 1945, he says, the Russian bear's paws have been "caught in an East European trap"—a characterization which prompted one left-wing French writer to respond derisively, "Now isn't that touching! The poor bear is so clumsy that its paws always . . . manage to stumble into traps . . . ."[72]

Bahro also sympathetically describes the Kremlin leaders as men "quite serious about feeling misunderstood" by the West. Systematic Soviet

---

[69]*Pakt*, p. 6.
[70]*Ibid.*, p. 50.
[71]*FM*, p. 2.
[72]André Gorz, "What, Then, is Freedom? Reply to Bahro," *Telos*, Spring 1982, p. 127.

violations of the Helsinki accords go unremarked, while such names as Sakharov and the Gulag make very rare appearances in Green statements. Soviet military involvement in Third World countries is only a frustrated effort to play "catch up" with the West. Soviet allies in Afghanistan acted with "good intentions" to bring reform, while the Soviet intervention was a blunder ("a role we never wanted them to play"), disturbing primarily in that it justified the claims of Western ruling circles for more arms.[73] The Soviet arms buildup is meant to "secure" their own bloc and not to threaten the West, while the SS-20 is dangerous only in that it will be "a propagandistic excuse" for a Western response.

To reinforce their notion of a mutual power struggle as the dynamic of East-West tension and thus the arms race, the Greens distort U.S. policy. They blame Washington for taking each new step in the arms race during the postwar period because it allegedly sought to maintain its immediate postwar strategic superiority, when, in fact, the United States made many advances merely because its technology was superior to that of the Soviets. But now that the United States is striving to redress the military balance in Europe, the Greens attack U.S. Pershing II missiles, which can destroy only about 54 targets, as "first-strike" weapons; mislabel NATO's declarative "first-use" policy as a "first-strike" posture; and accuse America of disrupting the "arms balance" even though no such thing is considered possible in the Greens' worldview. In general, "the peace today is threatened above all by the expansionist policy of the U.S.A.," not the Soviet Union.

To help blur distinctions between the blocs, Green programs stir up a sense of national victimization among fellow Germans. Ignoring their country's own past and overlooking its very brief period as a completely unified state (1871-1945), they declare that Germany has been divided unnaturally by the superpowers, which are intent solely on carrying out their power struggle. This notion is reinforced by paranoid charges of "backstabbing" and "betrayal" aimed at the Western allies. The Federal Republic and Berlin are "exploited" by America, which continues to "prolong its occupation" of both. Washington plans to use the country as "a staging area" and a "battlefield" and—like the Soviet Union—"will never give away" its half of Germany, but will instead reserve it for use in the "power struggle." In Berlin the Western allies continue to run roughshod over the inhabitants and "deny them their elementary human rights."[74]

---

[73]Bahro, *Socialism and Survival, op. cit.*, pp. 53-55.
[74]*Pakt*, p. 22.

When combined with its tendency to equate the superpowers, the movement's sense of victimization leads it to draw unconvincing parallels between East and West Germany. Bonn's liberal system and East Berlin's dictatorial police state are called "the same" by Petra Kelly, with only minor differences.[75] Both states allegedly block social change and "threaten democratic rights and freedoms."[76] To support this charge, they cite the example of Bonn's law forbidding members of avowed radical groups to hold public jobs, which affects a few hundred political extremists, and compare it with East Germany's across-the-board quashing of dissent and free expression. The latter instances of repression are said to be merely "more visible." In foreign policy, too, the German states are both described as puppets. The Greens compare the GDR's armed intervention to help Moscow crush the 1968 Prague Spring with U.S. "threats" to use the FRG's Bundeswehr in defense "of American oil interests in the mideast."[77]

As part of this victimization fiction, the Greens tend to embellish their own role by depicting themselves as the Western equivalents of Soviet-bloc groups fighting for independence. The Greens claim that the independent Polish Trade Union, Solidarity, represents their own principles of "social justice, basis democracy and nonviolence," but downplay the fact that the Poles are struggling for the same basic rights of free expression that the Greens enjoy but take for granted. Indeed, many Green members seem to want to provoke a government crackdown with their protest tactics so that this equating of conditions in the two blocs might appear to have at least some validity.

### Green Alternatives for the West

The Greens declare that there cannot be permanent peace and a liveable world until the movement's own leitmotifs are treated as fundamental criteria for policy. International relations must be based on social, ecological "basis" democratic and nonviolent standards as the Greens define them.

In what they term as concrete steps toward a *blockfrei, atomwaffenfrei* world, the Greens would start with entirely unilateral, unconditional "calculated concessions in the realm of trust-building measures." Foremost among these would be nuclear disarmament "which must begin in one's

---

[75]Petra Kelly, "Das System ist bankrott," *op. cit.*, p. 128.
[76]*Pakt*, p. 7.
[77]*Ibid.*, p. 55.

own land and should induce other countries likewise to disarm."[78] Thus, the Greens call for Bonn's rejection of any new nuclear weapons—above all, NATO's INF modernization program—without making such a move contingent upon the results of superpower arms talks. They would then declare West Germany a nuclear free zone and demand removal of all nuclear weapons from its territory. It is claimed that such unilateral measures will encourage other NATO allies to follow suit, creating the climate of trust necessary for broader East-West progress toward nuclear free zones, covering first both Germanys and eventually all of Europe.

The Greens believe this "cycle of disarmament" will reverse the arms race altogether. Citing Britain's unilateralist Bertrand Russell Foundation, they declare "a Europe that is free of atomic weapons, including in its surrounding seas, will liberate the Soviet Union from a grave threat and facilitate the equally necessary complete dismantling of the middle range rockets aimed at Western Europe."[79] With this "pressure" on Moscow alleviated, it is held that overall East-West disarmament will ensue, especially since the process of unilateral concessions, followed by multilateral agreements, will "strengthen the peace movements" and thus "assist in a breakthrough to worldwide disarmament, above all by the United States and the Soviet Union."[80] While disarming, the Greens would also begin dissolving West German ties with NATO, first by denying the Alliance use of the Federal Republic's territory for chemical/biological weapons deployment, airfields and overflight, maneuvers, and finally troops themselves. Such a departure will, they claim, provide a special incentive for dismantling the entire bloc system:

> The way to a bloc-free Europe [includes] the step-by-step loosening of the Federal Republic from NATO—exactly because the Federal Republic distinct from other West European countries plays the role of a specially loyal Alliance partner of the USA. Instead of placing its territory at the convenience of the hegemonial efforts and the offensive strategy of the US and thus delivering itself up to atomic destruction, the Federal Republic must pull out of all NATO measures and represent its own vital interests vis-a-vis the USA.[81]

The Greens assert that a nonnuclear FRG, free from "bloc bondage," would set in motion a process culminating in a more secure and stable peace for all Europe and thus the world. To begin with, the Greens assert that a nonaligned Federal Republic could propose mutual *bloc-freiheit* with its German neighbor, claiming that "an offer of bloc-free status could

---

[78]*BP* (Europäische Friedenspolitik), p. 19.
[79]*FM*, p. 10.
[80]*BP* (Europäische Friedenspolitik), p. 19.
[81]*FM*, p. 10.

not be ignored by the GDR and the rest of the East bloc." Their propagandistic *Feindbild* of the revanchist, reactionary [West] Germans would collapse."[82] Bloc-free status "can also gain for Berlin a new perspective on the future." Both Germanys would move rapidly toward complete demilitarization of society, eventually abolishing everything from the weapons industry and the armed forces to children's war games and toys and military monuments. In addition, any institutions in West German society which promote the creation of a *Feindbilder*—an image of an enemy—must be done away with.

The Greens would adopt an entirely defensive posture—a system adequate to protect the country and thus stave off any potential attackers, but not capable of threatening neighboring states. "In particular, the population of East Europe must be shown, not only that an offensive from the FRG will not be waged, but that it cannot be waged."[83] This "purely defensive" concept does not merely ban all potentially offensive weapons, but consists largely of "social defense"—a completely nonmilitary means of protection. This approach is said to be consistent with the movement's emphasis on nonviolence, although some Greens doubt its ultimate effectiveness. "Social defense" is defined as nonviolent acts of solidarity designed to frustrate an internal putsch as well as an external invasion, and specifically envisions "well-coordinated civil disobedience"—legal protest, demonstrations, strikes, boycotts, blockades, sabotage, breaking communication lines, "influencing" occupation troops, and guerrilla war against nonhuman targets. The concept is designed to preserve "our form of life" and "social institutions," not territory. An aggressive foreign power would see that "occupation and control would bring them more difficulties and burdens than increased power and profit."[84] Training in social defense will "ensure" that this nonviolent resistance will succeed where other efforts have failed.

A demilitarized, nonaligned German confederation, including Berlin, could undermine the bloc system entirely, thereby removing what the Greens see as the major cause of potential conflict in Europe—American and Soviet forces standing face-to-face at the continent's center. Because this development "lies in the interests" of all other European states, and because a "bloc-free" Germany as pictured by the Greens would heed the call of nonviolence, other European countries would welcome these developments. A demilitarized Central Europe, furthermore, would induce

---

[82]*Pakt*, p. 19.
[83]*FM*, p. 13.
[84]*BP* (Europäische Friedenspolitik), p. 19.

Moscow to loosen its grip on Eastern Europe and eventually permit the East Europeans "to liberate themselves":[85]

The convincing proof of the reduction of the threat to the Soviet Union from the Western Alliance and its front states will enable the Soviet Union in the future to hold back from such interventions [as in Czechoslovakia] and simultaneously permit the movements for independence in these countries another argument in their struggle.[86]

Thus, the groundwork can be laid for "overcoming the division of Europe," "all foreign troops [could be] withdrawn from foreign territory," and the last wounds of the Cold War healed. In the process, the nonalignment of the German states would be transformed into a confederation and eventually a reunified, demilitarized state. The Greens claim Moscow could tolerate this, just as it once quickly accepted the idea of an "independent, sovereign, neutral Austria," especially since this Germany need not be a centralized Bismarckian state, but primarily a "cultural, economic and humane entity" and a demilitarized state threatening to no one.[87]

The movement expresses its confidence that this process dissolving the blocs will not stop with Europe, but will "heighten the chance of peace and freedom worldwide." Movement away from bloc confrontation in Europe will weaken the position of the superpowers, remove their excuse for intervention elsewhere, and strengthen the right of self-determination of poorer, exploited Third World countries. A demilitarized Europe will have more money for foreign aid and produce no arms for export. Green visions of development also presuppose massive socioeconomic reform in Europe; burdens on the poor countries will be eased if the Federal Republic—and other industrialized countries following its example—consumes and pollutes less, while developing environmentally-safe, labor-intensive production methods and reducing the extent of corporate technological power over the world economy. Third World debt will be canceled, and all strings removed from aid. The Greens' foreign aid efforts would promote land reform, along with modern, ecological, labor-intensive, regional-specific development, and provide the necessary education and training programs. Support for large-scale, high-technology projects and military hardware would end. Goods from poor countries must receive a guaranteed "fair price" and eventually they should be freed from "the world market." As far as private involvement in development, the Greens claim that multinational firms' links with the Third World must be curtailed and eventually severed.

---

[85]Bahro, "The SPD and the Peace Movement," *op. cit.*, p. 22.
[86]*Ham.*
[87]*Pakt,* pp. 53, 14.

Although the Green world system would begin with unilateral measures, it also foresees the strengthening of the United Nations and the removal of the superpower veto. The world body would oversee global disarmament, economic development, ecological safeguards, space exploration, birth control, protection of human rights, and implementation of nonviolence and "soft technology."

## Evaluating the Alternatives

That same myopia which blurs the movement's view of the real world today also afflicts its vision of how international relations should be transformed; in both cases, the Greens' perspective is clouded by a deep-seated contempt for their own society. They advocate policies which assume that the world's ills can be alleviated only by a new mentality in the West. Theirs is a program which, taking for granted the importance and uniqueness of the West's open system, naively implies that all governments can be compelled to change course under the pressure of peaceful protest and public opinion. This fundamental misapprehension, coupled with a mortal dread of nuclear deterrence, prompts them to advance wildly improbable schemes for securing peace and development.

It is not surprising that the Greens advocate unilateral Western disarmament and West German withdrawal from NATO as key steps in reducing world tension. Because they lump East and West together as "industrialized systems" locked in superpower rivalry based on sheer ambition, the Greens believe Western concessions will remove further pressure on Moscow to keep up with its foe. This formula hardly accounts for the primary dynamics of Kremlin policy: the need to compensate for the Soviet system's economic failures and repression in the Soviet bloc by pursuing an assertive external policy that includes intimidating neighbors and setting up pro-Soviet regimes. If Moscow's military policy is, as the Greens claim, defensive in nature, it is one designed not so much to defend the Soviet empire from its rival's military might, but rather to defend the Soviet system from pressure for change—a goal best achieved by Soviet aggression abroad. It would be unthinkable for Moscow to imitate Western disarmament, as the Greens imagine. Since it is the Kremlin's military power and the resultant superpower status that preserve the Soviet system, Moscow would surely exploit the opportunities presented by an unarmed West, by retaining a military advantage sufficient to intimidate its neighbors and by creating instability in the rival camp, and thus securing its own position. Incredibly enough, the Greens adduce as evidence of the Soviet willingness to disarm the repeated Kremlin offers of a Nordic nuclear-free zone, which, as Moscow outlines it, requires only Western countries to dismantle weapons. At any rate, there is empirical evidence to indicate that Western concessions would be unlikely to prompt Soviet reciprocation: The period marking the greatest expansion of Soviet military power (even after SALT II which they claimed would "ratify parity") was the 1970s, when the West did little to modernize its military forces and was retreating from global involvement.

Nor, as the Greens assert, would unilateral German steps to dissolve NATO allow Moscow to ease its grip on Eastern Europe so that the satellite countries could "liberate themselves" and eventually help create a bloc-free Europe, as well as a sovereign, independent, democratic and reunified Germany. For permitting all of Central Europe and eventually Eastern Europe to be liberated of pro-Moscow regimes would only further expose the entire Soviet system to the attraction of Western institutions and values—a greater threat than lingering German militarism, which the Greens claim their plan would eliminate. Precisely this threat of destabilization of their system would prompt Moscow to tighten, rather than weaken, its grip over Eastern Europe. As Pierre Hassner points out, any hope of destabilizing the Soviet bloc presupposes protected "rear ranks" in the Western camp.[88]

The Greens become further mired in their own basic misunderstanding of the systemic differences between East and West by insisting that NATO disarmament will destroy the Kremlin's carefully fabricated *Feindbilder* of an aggressive West and thereby compel Moscow to follow suit, "to placate its own public opinion."[89] Similarly, they claim to believe that Bonn's unilateral disarmament and withdrawal from NATO will destroy the GDR's *Feindbild* of a revanchist West Germany and lead East German citizens to demand that their government reciprocate, creating a nuclear-free, bloc-free Germany. This hypothesis vastly overrates the susceptibility of the Soviet camp's foreign policy to "grass roots" control. Even if Soviet and all East European citizens came to disbelieve entirely their rulers' *Feindbilder* of the West, their opinions are not likely to alter Kremlin policy. Currently, Poles and Czechs hardly "support" the Warsaw Pact because of any fear of Western invasion, and any hope that their attitudes will shake apart the Soviet bloc military apparatus is illusory.

At any rate, the suggestion that Western disarmament would be clearly perceived by Eastern publics as ending the need for a Soviet world role disregards the power of closed societies to manipulate the images their

---

[88]Pierre Hassner, "Defense, Human Rights & Detente: A Dialogue with Viveret," *Telos*, Spring 1982, p. 114.

[89]Rudolf Bahro, "The SPD and the Peace Movement," *op: cit.*, p. 21.

populations have of world events. To the extent it needs to retain credibility for its foreign policy, the Kremlin would simply declare that Western unilateral disarmament marked a great victory for the socialist camp, while at the same time continuing to create the impression of a need for world revolution—to help fraternal socialists and to forestall a revival of "imperialism." Moscow would create the tension it requires to preserve its rule; after all, unilateral West German disarmament and neutralism would produce a power vacuum inviting Soviet involvement that could further the Kremlin's ambitions.

In short, a Western policy of unilateral disarmament, neutralism and even complete demilitarization, as the Greens advocate, would not encourage the Kremlin to reciprocate; quite the opposite is true. So long as a Western world with the real threat of a democratic virus exists, Moscow—given its system—must and can sustain a policy of confrontation. Indirectly, the Greens acknowledge this by advocating such complete disarmament and demilitarization as to dismantle entirely Western *Feindbilder* of the Soviet bloc. Presumably "political antagonism" toward the Kremlin and even rhetorical support for liberty in Eastern Europe would violate the spirit of accommodation, as the Greens perceive it. In short, to ensure the success of their unilateral political and military disarmament, the Greens would complement it with psychological disarmament.

The Greens' program is dangerous as well as naive. Although they insist that a denuclearized, neutralized, demilitarized Germany and bloc-free Europe would eliminate all possible sources of conflict, Moscow's intrinsic need to maintain superpower status and forestall systemic change in its own camp would require Soviet interference in a "Green Europe." If the "Prague Spring" necessitated swift Kremlin action to eradicate a potential democratic virus, how much easier and more tempting it would be to stifle possible political contagion from a free but disarmed Western Europe. The Greens declare that their country would be a democratic socialist state threatening no one; it is precisely this condition that would prompt Soviet efforts to exercise military and political control over Germany. At the very least, the shadow of unmatched Soviet military might looming on the horizon would "Finlandize" Germany and Europe with it, a relationship Yuri Andropov considers the epitome of detente.

This is where "social defense" comes in, another concept spawned by the movement's tendency to equate the blocs and to discount the West's unique openness. So acclimated are the Greens to life in a liberal society that they take its openness for granted, and demonstrate a naive faith in the universal applicability of tactics that have allowed them successfully to influence West German public opinion. They claim these measures can be extended to foreign relations, and that the Germans could thus deter any aggressor by threatening to act uncooperatively, to use non-violent protest, to strike, to sabotage—a pathetically utopian assumption. Defying all historical evidence, the Greens assert that "a nation cannot be long ruled if it is not ready to cooperate with its oppressor."[90] They qualify this statement by saying people must be prepared beforehand to resist in solidarity, though Germany's neighbor Poland, a country of remarkable cohesion, has enjoyed only a scant few decades of independence in the past several centuries. In a sense, the Greens themselves live in a country littered with monuments to the failure of nonviolent resistance. But since the movement declares that "the Americans staying" will prove worse than "the Russians coming," they believe social defense is worth any risk.

## Conclusion

Political platforms are never paradigms of clarity and detached analysis; the Greens' is no exception. Indeed, the coherence and conceptual credibility of their program is particularly weak because the Greens are a movement rather than a party, a movement which tolerates the whims of its heterogeneous, grass roots "basis."

But such considerations can only partly explain why the Green program is characterized by convoluted reasoning and tortured logic, cataclysmic hyperbole and disingenuous blame-laying, hazy visions and unworkable proposals. It is clear that Green policy statements owe almost everything to instinct and little to analysis. The movement has tried to channel the powerful but inchoate sentiments of its members into positions on policy, with little success. In the end, evaluating the Green program is important far more because of what it indicates about these impulses than because the program itself has practical merits or stands any chance of being implemented.

Some of the feelings that have shaped their policy statements are easy to sympathize with. Above all, the movement's basic fears are valid and understandable; no West German could deny that his countrymen have particular cause for concern about environmental deterioration and nuclear weapons, among other things. Moreover, the movement's policy concepts also reflect a strong dose of understandable if unrealistic and dangerous wishful thinking, such as the desire to believe that industrialization's side effects and nuclear deterrence are symptoms of a horrible disease that can be quickly cured without taking on greater risks in the process.

---

[90]*FM*, p. 12.

But far more significant than the Greens' feelings of severe pessimism toward the present and over-optimism about their program for the future are certain unmistakable negative instincts, many of which bespeak a neo-romantic reaction against rationality and reality. The program's critique of the world it lives in involves an exaggerated, unreasoning contempt for modernism, a sense of victimization, and a self-righteous moralism. These tendencies are summed up by Rudolf Bahro's plea for change "before the Great Machine has completely regulated us, concreted over us, poisoned us, asphyxiated us, and sooner or later subjected us to total nuclear annihilation."[91] These are the same instincts which characterized past waves of romanticism, particularly "cultural despair," a highly political form of romanticism which loathed parliamentary politics, bourgeois capitalism and technological society. Like earlier romantics, the Greens direct their contempt against both domestic and external enemies. And it is ironic that the movement which calls upon German leaders to act in the belief that all men are essentially good, and to dismantle *Feindbilder* of the Soviets, has clearly cultivated its own *Feindbilder:* it castigates members of the Establishment, who are depicted in one critic's words as "ruthless destroyers of the prospect of a good, healthy, happy, clean-lunged life," and condemn traitorously conspiring politicians who sell out the homeland to even more venal foes, the Americans, who manipulate Germany from abroad.[92]

With regard to solutions, the Green program is eclectic in its impracticality, borrowing the slogans or echoing the sentiments of utopian socialism, anarchism and Marxism without fully incorporating the overall theoretical formulas of any one tradition. Again, the major common thread of the movement's program is provided by the romantic instinct for escapism, to make that "leap from despair to utopia across all existing reality." Scorning any short-term, pragmatic, limited changes, they insist that the transformation must be fundamental, systemic, attitudinal—nothing short of a new mentality, a new man.

For all these reasons, because they conjure up certain unmistakable nationalist sentiments, and because their reactionary romanticism blends elements of the Right and Left, the Greens have aroused recollections of Nazism and Fascism, two movements which in similar as well as separate ways exploited romantic impulses. Whatever the ultimate validity of such parallels, the Greens' basic contempt for the modern West blinds them to its virtues, not just to reality; the solutions they put forward for today's

---

[91]Bahro, *Socialism & Survival, op. cit.*, p.142.
[92]Helmut Schoeck, "Letter from Germany: Protesting for a Brave, Green World," '*Encounter,* December 1982, p. 50.

problems, in order to escape from the not always pleasant real world, would undermine free, democratic Western institutions. As one Social Democrat put it, they risk creating "a generation of anti-democratic, anti-socialist, elite-bourgeois dropouts,"[93] and ultimately they arrive at the conclusion that preserving Western Civilization as it is currently constituted would not be worth risking anyone's survival. When French leftist intellectual Andre Gorz responded to Rudolf Bahro by declaring "I can no longer see what you basically stand for, i.e., what values make you find life worth living,"[94] he characterized the movement's mindset as revealed by its program. Pure survival seems to be the only ethical end, because they have turned their backs on Western society and institutions.

---

[93]Klaus Matthiesen, cited in Scharping and Hofmann-Göttig, *op. cit.*, p. 401.
[94]Gorz, *op. cit.*, p. 127.

# The Greens/Alternatives and the Peace Movement: A Challenge to the German Party System

## by Werner Kaltefleiter

### The Greens/Alternatives: A Uniquely German Movement?

The Green/Alternative movement is presently attracting considerable attention on the German political scene. What does this group's emergence mean for the stability of democracy in the Federal Republic of Germany? What are its historical roots? Does it derive from certain unique features of German political culture? Especially since the merger of the Greens/Alternatives with the peace movement, questions have been raised with regard to West Germany's future position in the Atlantic Alliance. Some even ask if the Federal Republic is going neutral. Even after the significant victory of the CDU/CSU-FDP coalition under the leadership of Chancellor Helmut Kohl on March 6, 1983, these questions are still raised, though not as frequently in the Federal Republic as in other countries of the Western world.

To understand the new political formation represented by the Greens it must be realized that the parliamentary system in the Federal Republic of Germany, as in all other continental European democracies except France, is based on proportional representation. In the Federal Republic the principle of proportional representation is modified by a 5 percent threshold, which means that a party has to gain at least 5 percent of the total vote to qualify for seats in parliament. The simple implication of this electoral system—which is practiced in municipal, state and federal elections—is that splinter parties, which would rarely be a factor under the Anglo-Saxon plurality system of single-member districts, may send representatives to parliament in Bonn. In the United States, for example, a presidential candidate need only obtain more votes than any one of his opponents to take all of the electoral votes of a state. The same principle holds in American Congressional contests and in British Parliamentary elections. Although the United States deeply influenced the constitutional development of West Germany after World War II, it did not attempt to impose the plurality system.

The Greens claim that our world today is challenged by problems that no previous generation has confronted: the alleged threat to all mankind posed by the pollution of air, water and earth in industrialized societies, and the supposed menace of nuclear energy and nuclear weapons. Such threats are said to justify the new forms of political participation which include unconventional methods of civil disobedience, even the use of violence. It is especially this commitment to civil disobedience that differentiates the Greens from various "return to nature" movements of the past; they shared some more or less romantic visions of a new life-style, but not the political action program of the Greens/Alternatives. Therefore, in trying to understand the Greens and their implications for German politics, historical parallels have only limited utility.

The Greens/Alternatives are a part of the politics of the Federal Republic of Germany, but they are similar to movements in the Scandinavian countries, the Netherlands, France and Britain. And the fusion between the ecological movement and the peace movement in West Germany has its counterpart in other European countries: for example, the Greens' famous slogan, "nuclear energy no thanks," originated in Sweden.

## The Structure of the Greens/Alternatives

From an organizational point of view, the Green movement consists of four concentric circles. The innermost circle of activists contains no more than about 20,000 people, who can be divided into two segments. First, there are the "true believers," a heterogeneous group, many of whose members are affiliated with the Protestant Church and especially with its pietist wing. Second, the inner circle consists of followers of various communist groups which are also heterogeneous, but nevertheless of great importance to the organizational coherence of the Green/Alternative movement. In accordance with Lenin's theory of alliances, the communists try to gain under the green flag what they never achieved under the red flag: a position of political influence in the Federal Republic. The composition of the inner circle of the Greens varies from region to region, but in general a "50-50 split" describes fairly accurately the existing reality. This split also explains the composite name "Greens/Alternatives": the Greens are recruited mostly from the first group, the true believers; the Alternatives mostly from the second, the different communist groups.

The distribution of power between the two factions varies from region to region, and every "party convention" is characterized by the conflict between them—i.e., the true believers with ethical attitudes and communists of various kinds. The numerous contradictions in the party program derive from the conflict between them. To understand the operation of the Greens/Alternatives as a party, it is most important to examine the workings of its inner circle. Three elements characterize its organizational structure, which is dominated by the concept of "decentralized democracy," that is, an emphasis on "grass roots" control over decisionmaking:

(1) The convention of all members in a certain region or the convention of delegates on the federal level takes the final decision on all issues, which are binding on all Green members of state assemblies and the federal Parliament.

(2) The Greens are eager to avoid personal leadership. They elect only "speakers," who change frequently according to a rotation scheme. The principle of rotation is also applied to all Green members of Parliament, who are requested to resign in the middle of the legislative period. Since they are all elected on a party list, those who follow on the list succeed them in Parliament. (It should be noted that this practice is unconstitutional in the Federal Republic, but it cannot be predicted whether it will be tested in the courts.)

(3) The division between the true believers and the communists leads to the "zipper principle" in the recruitment of candidates for parliamentary seats: a candidate of the first group is followed by one of the second who is followed again by one of the first on the party list.

The social base of these inner circles is middle and upper-middle class. Teachers, social workers, other members of the civil service, and a few students dominate these groups. Working class people are largely unrepresented by the Greens/Alternatives.

Another concentric circle can be drawn around this inner circle, comprising approximately 200,000 people—those who are eventually willing to follow calls by the Greens/Alternatives to join demonstrations or other political activities. This number might be higher for some major demonstrations—for example, in the fall of 1981—because they can often rely on support from similar groups in other European countries.

The third circle consists of those who are prepared to support the Green/Alternative movement in elections but do not take part in mass meetings and political demonstrations. This circle may amount to 8-10 percent of the population, and it consists chiefly of persons up to 30 years of age, with a high level of education, and belonging to the middle, the upper-middle, and the upper classes. Non-Catholics and residents of urbanized areas are also strongly represented among the Green/Alternative vote (See Table 1.)

Finally, there is a fourth circle consisting of about 40 percent of the electorate. These individuals do not share the views of the Greens and are not prepared to vote for them, but they welcome their existence as a warning to the established parties. It is interesting to note that three of

## TABLE 1
## The Structure of the Green/Alternative Electorate, 1983[1]

| Categories of Voters | Percentage of Voters Intending to Vote for the Greens/Alternatives |
|---|---|
| All Eligible Voters | 6.0 |
| **By Class** | |
| Working class | 4.5 |
| Middle class | 5.1 |
| Upper class | 12.4 |
| **By Church Attendance** | |
| Catholic | 0.8 |
| Protestant | 3.2 |
| Neither | 7.3 |
| **By Church Affiliation** | |
| Catholic | 4.2 |
| Protestant | 5.3 |
| Others | 7.4 |
| No affiliation | 19.6 |
| **By Area of Residence** | |
| Rural | 2.5 |
| Township | 4.5 |
| Urban | 12.8 |
| **By Last Educational Level Attained** | |
| Primary school | 2.3 |
| High school | 6.4 |
| College | 17.1 |
| **By Age Group** | |
| 18-24 | 15.4 |
| 25-29 | 20.2 |
| 30-39 | 6.1 |
| 40-49 | 1.6 |
| 50-59 | 2.0 |
| Over 60 | 0.2 |
| **By Sex** | |
| Male | 6.5 |
| Female | 5.3 |

[1]This table shows the percentage of voters in different social categories who expressed an intention to vote for the Greens in early 1983.

these circles, the cadre, the demonstrators, and the "hidden sympathizers"—circles 1, 2 and 4—have been rather stable in size during the last four years since the Green movement gained momentum. (See Table 2.)

## The Greens/Alternatives as an Ecological Group: The First Phase

The evolution of the Green/Alternative movement may be divided into two phases. Initially, it was oriented toward specific regional or local cases of ecological/environmental damage, such as organizing protests against the felling of trees or the pollution of waters. Later, issues were added which attracted broader attention and transcended local-regional differences among the different Green/Alternative groups. The best examples of this second phase were the protests against nuclear power stations and later against the construction of a new runway at the Frankfurt Airport. During this phase, the Greens/Alternatives merged with the "peace movement," and found a major national issue in the protest against the NATO dual-track decision of December 1979 and especially the deployment of intermediate-range missiles in Europe. During the campaign for the federal election of March 6, 1983, the protest against the possible deployment of intermediate-range missiles dominated all other issues which were of interest to the Green/Alternative movement.

This shift from emphasis on local to nationwide issues was clearly reflected in the evolution of the Green/Alternative voting base. When they first appeared on the political stage in the municipal elections in Schleswig-Holstein in 1978, and only a short time later in the state elections in Lower Saxony, the Greens/Alternatives focused mainly on controversial local projects. When they got their first seat in the county council of Steinburg/Schleswig-Holstein, they won over 15 percent of the votes close to the planned nuclear power station at Brokdorf, but only about 2-3 percent in the rest of the county. A similar pattern could be discerned in the county of Nordfriesland and in the state election in Lower Saxony. In the latter election, the Greens/Alternatives won almost 30 percent of the vote close to Grohnde and Gorleben, where nuclear installations have been planned; in the rest of the state, however, they obtained no more than 3-4 percent.

As a consequence of focusing on specific issues of a highly localized nature, the Green/Alternative movement drew votes from the ranks of all parties. In the strongholds of the Greens, i.e., close to controversial projects as, for example, nuclear power stations, the CDU, SPD and FDP lost almost equally to the new political group. Accordingly, in 1979 and into 1980, the Greens/Alternatives were perceived incorrectly to be a movement belonging to the political center. On the left-right continuum ranging from 5 points to the left to 5 points to the right, the Greens at that

## TABLE 2
### Attitudes toward the Greens, According to Voting Intentions

| Questions | Answers | Year | All respondants | Voting Intention[1] | | | |
|---|---|---|---|---|---|---|---|
| | | | | CDU/CSU | SPD | FDP | Greens |
| Do you favor the Greens' decision to compete in the election? | Yes, I find it desirable | 1978 | 44.1 | 38.4 | 44.8 | 48.7 | — |
| | | 1980 | 43.5 | 32.1 | 47.8 | 45.9 | — |
| | | 1983 | 43.5 | 27.6 | 55.5 | 56.8 | 95.4 |
| | No, I do not find it desirable | 1978 | 55.9 | 61.6 | 55.2 | 51.3 | — |
| | | 1980 | 56.5 | 67.9 | 52.2 | 54.1 | — |
| | | 1983 | 56.5 | 72.4 | 44.5 | 43.2 | 4.6 |
| Which of the following evaluations about the Greens' participation in the election is closest to your own view? | Their participation is necessary: Other parties are too far removed from citizen's daily lives and problems | 1978 | 37.3 | 31.5 | 37.4 | 42.7 | — |
| | | 1980 | 31.4 | 22.2 | 33.7 | 38.9 | — |
| | | 1983 | 37.6 | 20.6 | 49.6 | 43.3 | 91.3 |
| | meaningless: they will not enter the Bundestag | 1978 | 33.9 | 36.9 | 34.2 | 29.5 | — |
| | | 1980 | 44.2 | 51.3 | 42.4 | 38.3 | — |
| | | 1983 | 26.6 | 30.0 | 26.7 | 11.9 | 6.1 |
| | dangerous: they will fragment the party system | 1978 | 28.8 | 31.7 | 28.4 | 27.8 | — |
| | | 1980 | 24.4 | 26.5 | 23.9 | 22.8 | — |
| | | 1983 | 35.8 | 49.5 | 23.8 | 44.7 | 2.6 |
| Attitude toward voting for the Greens: | will not vote for them, satisfied with other parties: | 1983 | 38.1 | 48.6 | 33.1 | 31.6 | 2.6 |
| | will not vote for them despite dissatisfaction with other parties | 1983 | 37.2 | 40.0 | 37.1 | 50.8 | 1.7 |
| | Unlikely, but critical of other parties | 1983 | 9.9 | 5.6 | 13.4 | 10.8 | 9.8 |
| | conceivable that I will vote for the Greens | 1983 | 9.9 | 5.3 | 14.8 | 6.6 | 13.1 |
| | rather certain that I will vote for the Greens | 1983 | 4.8 | 0.6 | 1.6 | 0.3 | 72.8 |

[1]CDU/CSU-Christian Democratic Union/Christian Socialist Union; SPD-Social Democratic Party; FDP-Free Democratic Party; Greens-the Green Party

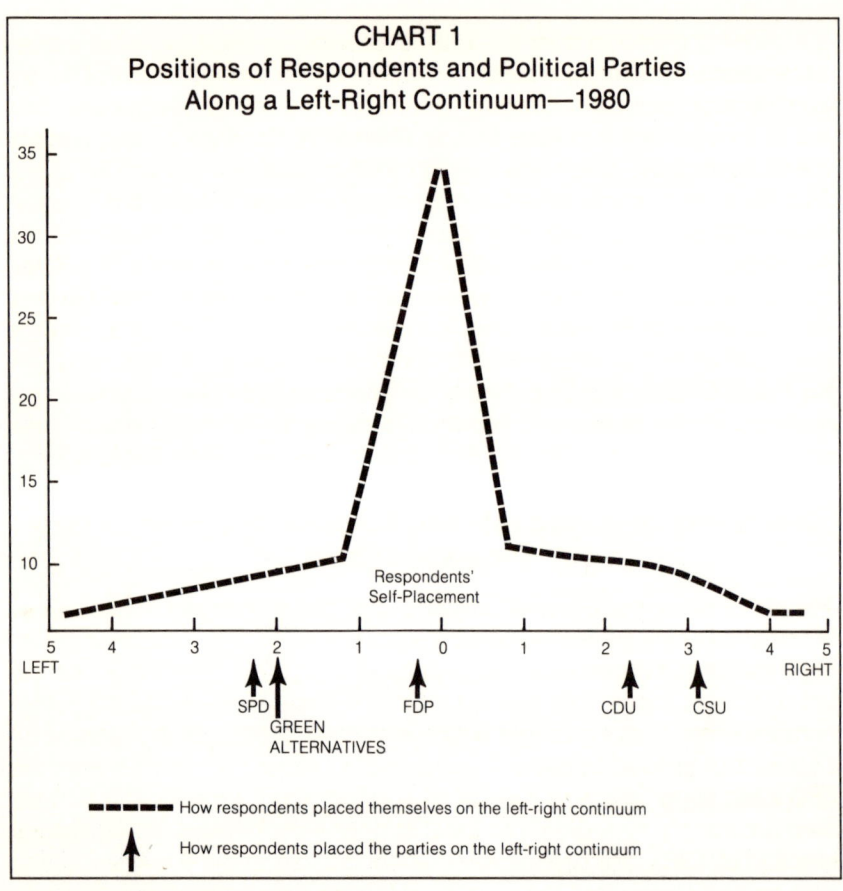

time in the perception of the electorate, as measured in public opinion polling, were given a "left 2.0" position in 1980, which is a moderate ranking close to the SPD. In Lower Saxony in 1978 they were even placed at a centrist "left 0.2" position. (See Chart 1.)

The initial successes of the Greens/Alternatives still reflected the two different groups that comprised their inner circle. In the election of 1978 their gains were based on the protest against specific local projects that were perceived to be damaging to the environment, or they were a consequence of the high percentage of students in the urbanized region. Among students there was great concern about environmental problems, which soon led to a general questioning of the value system of industrialized society. The belief in modern technology as an instrument to improve living conditions was increasingly opposed, and resistance to nuclear energy was only the tip of the iceberg: it became a symbol for the questioning of modern technology in general. In addition, other values such as economic reward based on achievement, the fulfillment of duties, and the importance of individual responsibility came to be opposed. This led to an alternative culture and an alternative life-style among parts of the student body, which was joined by other people in urbanized areas. This life-style became mixed with forms of behavior from the old "hippie" movement of the period of student unrest in the late 1960s, and the emphasis on an alternative culture contributed to the name "the Alternatives" as descriptive of the whole movement. The entry of the Greens/Alternatives into Bremen's state parliament in the fall of 1979, into the state parliament of Baden-Württemberg in the spring of 1980, and into the Berlin Chamber of Deputies in the spring of 1981, were stages in the maturing of the movement into an alternative to the major established political parties of the Federal Republic of Germany. (See Table 3.)

## Greens/Alternatives as a Left-Wing Fundamental Opposition Party: The Second Phase

The structure of the Green/Alternative electorate changed in the course of integrating the peace movement within its ranks. The Greens increasingly came to be perceived as a party of the Left in 1983 when, on the left-right continuum, they gained a left 3.4 position. (See Chart 2.) As a consequence, they no longer won substantial support from voters of all parties, but instead became a group that in effect had split off from the SPD's left wing. The structure of its support was characterized far less than previously by regional or local strongholds. Instead, in the federal election of 1983, the Greens/Alternatives gained about 5 percent of the vote spread throughout the country, retaining only a few of the old traditional strongholds. This new structure of electoral support was first seen in the state elections in Lower Saxony in March 1982, and has since been reflected in other elections, including those in Hamburg, Hesse and Bavaria, Rhineland-Palatinate and Schleswig-Holstein, and finally in the 1983 federal election.

However, one does not do the Green/Alternative movement justice by attributing its success solely to its advocacy of specific issues. The change in the structure of its electoral support suggests that it is a more complex phenomenon. In dealing with such political events, one must differentiate between how a party's appeal and electoral strength are affected by issues on the one hand, and by the structure and dynamics of the political system on the other hand.

The FDP notwithstanding, the German party system is a fundamentally dichotomized two-party system, the most characteristic dimension of

## TABLE 3
## Electoral Support of the Greens/Alternatives, 1978-1983
### (by percentage)

| Date of Election | Total Vote (%) | Regional Characteristics (%) | |
|---|---|---|---|
| March 1978<br>Municipal Election<br>Schleswig-Holstein | 0.7<br>(for several different<br>groups) | Steinburg<br>Nordfriesland | 6.6<br>6.0 |
| April 1979<br>State Election<br>Schleswig-Holstein | 2.4<br>(Green List Schleswig-<br>Holstein) | Steinburg-South | 5.4 |
| June 1978<br>State Election<br>Lower Saxony | 3.9<br>(Green List/<br>Environmental<br>Protection) | Hannover-Center<br>Hannover-List<br>Braunschweig-North-East<br>Lüchow-Dannenberg<br>Osnabrück-West<br>Göttingen<br>Hameln<br>Uelzen<br>Lüneburg<br>Cuxhaven<br>Jever<br>Wilhelmshaven | 5.5<br>4.9<br>6.0<br>13.4<br>5.2<br>5.9<br>5.2<br>6.8<br>6.3<br>6.4<br>5.9<br>5.1 |
| June 4, 1978<br>State Election<br>Hamburg | 4.6<br>(for three different<br>groups) | | |
| September 1979<br>State Election<br>Bremen | 1.4 (Alternatives)<br>5.1 (Greens) | | |
| March 1980<br>State Election<br>Baden-Württemberg | 5.3 | Stuttgart I<br>Tübingen<br>Freiburg I<br>Freiburg II<br>Heidelberg<br>Breisgau<br>Lörrach<br>Emmendingen<br>Konstanz<br>Waldshut | 6.9<br>9.9<br>11.2<br>11.6<br>8.1<br>9.8<br>7.8<br>7.7<br>7.7<br>7.4 |
| May 11, 1980<br>State Election<br>North Rhine-<br>Westphalia | 3.0<br>(Greens) | Köln I<br>Münster I<br>Bielefeld II | 6.0<br>5.8<br>5.0 |
| April 27, 1980<br>State Election<br>Saarland | 2.9<br>(Greens) | Gersheim | 5.4 |

Electoral Support of the Greens/Alternatives, 1978-1983
(by percentage)

| Date of Election | Total Vote (%) | Regional Characteristics (%) | |
|---|---|---|---|
| October 1980 Federal Election | 1.5 (Greens) | | |
| May 1981 State Election Berlin | 7.2 (Alternatives) | Tiergarten | 11.4 |
| | | Kreuzberg II | 17.4 |
| | | Kreuzberg III | 17.4 |
| | | Kreuzberg IV | 14.7 |
| | | Kreuzberg V | 18.2 |
| | | Charlottenburg IV | 11.7 |
| | | Charlottenburg V | 12.5 |
| | | Charlottenburg VI | 13.5 |
| | | Wilmersdorf | 10.9 |
| | | Schöneberg I | 12.7 |
| | | Schöneberg II | 16.9 |
| | | Schöneberg III | 11.0 |
| | | Schöneberg IV | 11.9 |
| | | Neukölln | 9.8 |
| March 1982 State Election Lower Saxony | 6.5 (Greens) | Braunschweig-North-East | 8.3 |
| | | Braunschweig-South-East | 7.0 |
| | | Braunschweig-South-West | 6.4 |
| | | Braunschweig-North-West | 6.4 |
| | | Göttingen | 11.7 |
| | | Hannover-Center | 9.9 |
| | | Hannover-North-East | 7.0 |
| | | Hannover-South-East | 7.1 |
| | | Hannover-Linden | 8.4 |
| | | Hannover-Limmer | 7.3 |
| | | Lüchow-Dannenberg | 14.1 |
| | | Osterholz-Scharmbeck | 9.2 |
| | | Lüneburg | 9.2 |
| | | Osnabrück-East | 6.6 |
| | | Osnabrück-West | 7.7 |
| | | Buchholz | 9.1 |
| | | Oldenburg-South | 10.9 |
| | | Oldenburg-North | 11.3 |
| | | Hameln | 7.0 |
| | | Hildesheim | 7.0 |
| | | Ammerland | 8.3 |
| | | Jever | 8.7 |
| | | Wilhelmshaven | 8.8 |
| June 1982 State Election Hamburg | 7.7 (Greens/Alternatives) | Eimsbüttel | 10.0 |

**Electoral Support of the Greens/Alternatives, 1978-1983**
(by percentage)

| Date of Election | Total Vote (%) | Regional Characteristics (%) | |
|---|---|---|---|
| September 1982<br>State Election<br>Hesse | 8.0<br>(Greens) | Frankfurt/M. II<br>Groβ-Gerau-East<br>Frankfurt/M. VIII<br>Darmstadt, Stadt I<br>Groβ-Gerau-West<br>Frankfurt/M. III | 19.5<br>18.2<br>15.0<br>14.3<br>12.5<br>12.1 |
| October 10, 1982<br>State Election<br>Bavaria | 4.6<br>(Greens) | München-Schwabing<br>München-Altstadt<br>München-Nymphenburg<br>Augsburg-Stadt | 10.0<br>8.9<br>7.9<br>6.5 |
| December 1982<br>State Election<br>Hamburg | 6.8<br>(Greens) | | |
| March 1983<br>Federal Election | 5.6<br>(Greens) | Heidelberg<br>Freiburg<br>Tübingen<br>München<br>Hamburg-Center<br>Hamburg-Altona<br>Hamburg-Eimsbüttel<br>Bremen-East<br>Münster<br>Frankfurt/M.<br>Stuttgart-South | 9.3<br>12.3<br>9.5<br>10.7<br>9.0<br>9.1<br>10.7<br>11.3<br>9.5<br>9.7<br>9.1 |
| March 1983<br>State Election<br>Rhineland-Palatinate | 4.5<br>(Greens) | Koblenz<br>Cochem-Zell<br>Trier<br>Kaiserslautern<br>Landau (Palatine)<br>Mainz<br>Speyer | 5.0<br>5.5<br>5.7<br>5.7<br>6.6<br>6.5<br>5.6 |
| March 1983<br>State Election<br>Schleswig-Holstein | 3.6<br>(Greens) | Südtondern<br>Kiel-Center<br>Norderstedt<br>Reinbek<br>Ahrensburg | 6.0<br>5.2<br>5.0<br>5.0<br>5.0 |

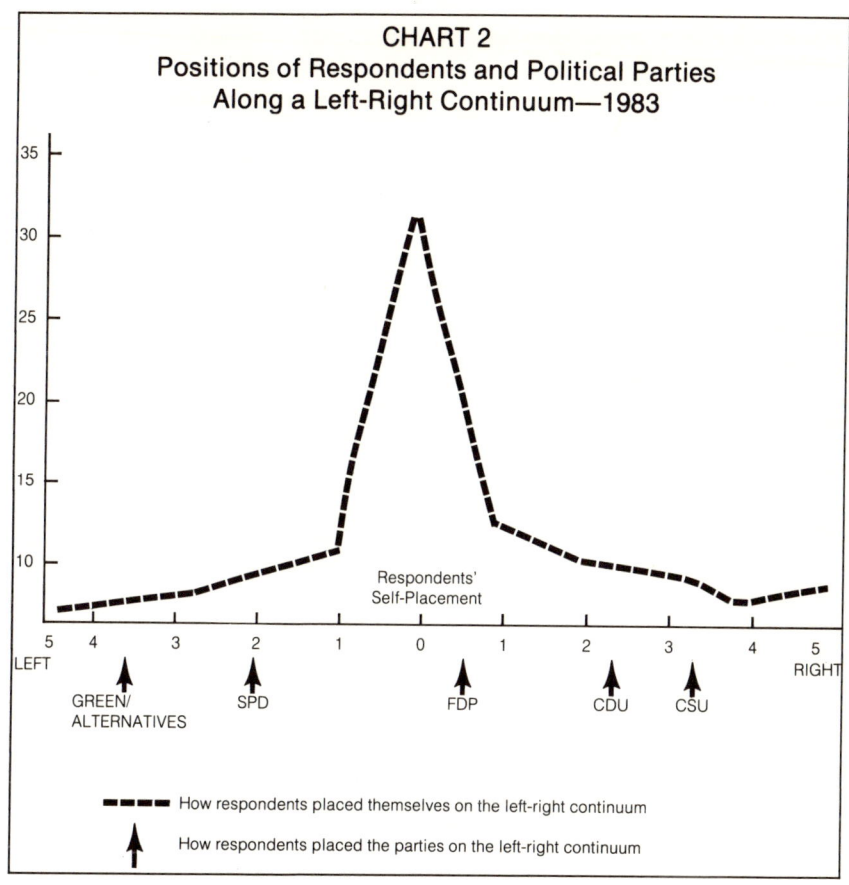

which is the struggle between change, on the one hand, and conservatism and stabilization, on the other. In such a system, one party always becomes the advocate of change, and the other the supporter of conservatism. This corresponds, respectively, to the general positions of the SPD and the CDU/CSU in the Federal Republic of Germany. In such a system, the task of the party of change is to integrate the restive elements of a modern industrialized society, which strive continually to effect change, whatever that might actually mean. Such change is mainly identified with economic redistribution.

In order to define the meaning of the party of change in the Federal Republic, it is important to understand the history of political ideas in Germany. With the establishment of the Federal Republic of Germany, the main principles of the political liberalism of the last century, i.e., constitutional government and a free market economy, became reality.

That led to a merging of conservative and liberal political thought. Conservative politics since that time has meant the defense of the political and economic order based on principles of nineteenth-century liberalism. In contrast, the SPD had always sought to change this order, and therefore became the party of change. It is useful to remember that in the Weimar Republic SPD party members marched through the streets carrying posters with the slogan, "A republic means little; socialism is the goal." Even in the Godesberg Program of 1959, by which the party sought to transform itself from a class party to a modern, more broadly based party, it was said democracy would become more perfect only by the introduction of socialism.

From time to time, however, situations arise in which the party of change is not in a position to integrate the restive segments of modern industrialized society. This was the case in the Federal Republic between 1966 and 1969, when the SPD formed the Grand Coalition with the CDU/CSU, which the most convinced followers of the SPD saw as a betrayal of the party's principles. A consequence was the rise of the so-called Extraparliamentary Opposition (APO) and the inner-party controversies within the SPD. It should be remembered that the Grand Coalition attracted support only from a very small majority in the SPD Nuremberg party convention in the spring of 1968, even though the SPD itself was a member of the coalition government and Willy Brandt was Foreign Minister.

The Grand Coalition did not last long enough for the Extraparliamentary Opposition to become a political force. Apart from the most loyal APO followers, the Grand Coalition was popular because it corresponded to a widespread desire for harmony and consensus within the electorate.

After the formation of the SPD/FDP coalition in 1969, the Extraparliamentary Opposition was temporarily reintegrated into the SPD, largely because of the high expectations that Willy Brandt created for the new coalition. "We are only at the beginning" and "dare more democracy" were illustrative of the slogans which expressed this overdrawn expectation of the government that he headed as Chancellor until 1974.

However, this integration of the Extraparliamentary Opposition into the SPD had two consequences. The first was the APO's transformation into an opposition *within* the party. As a result, the conflict between socialists and social democrats (that is, doctrinaire Marxists and more centrist reformers), which has been a part of the SPD's history since its foundation, broke out again with great acrimony and shaped the SPD's policy during the 1970s and into the present decade. Second, closely related was a slow but steady programmatic shift of the SPD to the left, which found its climax in the party convention in Munich in April 1982, and which was decisive in the breakup of the SPD/FDP coalition in the fall of 1982. Under the influence of its left wing, the SPD had moved away from the policy consensus that had sustained the governing coalition, though the party still formally furnished the chancellor.

More important for the Green/Alternative movement, however, was the fact that, as a governing party, the SPD was part of a coalition government with the FDP, subject to constraints that did not allow for the realization of drastic change. As a consequence, dissatisfaction with the SPD's policy soon began to grow again in the Left. Although they tried to change party policy by active participation in the internal decisionmaking process and although they were successful in shifting the party program more and more to the left, they could not influence greatly the policy of the SPD/FDP government. The change in 1974 from a more visionary Chancellor Willy Brandt to the considerably more pragmatic leadership of Helmut Schmidt was in this context of great symbolic importance. In 1972, the Young Socialists (the SPD's left-leaning youth organization) formed a torchlight procession for Willy Brandt after his success in the election, but they did not do this for Helmut Schmidt after his victory.

The left wing's frustration grew in the waning years of the SPD/FDP coalition. This frustration found various outlets. The first was the SPD's programmatic shift to the left already mentioned, which, however, did not influence the policy of the SPD government. The second manifestation was splits within the party. Most important, however, was the formation of the Green/Alternative movement, which recruited about 80 percent of its members from the SPD or from potential SPD followers. As a result, the Greens/Alternatives became a left-wing opposition party.

The following tables show how close those voters who identify with the Greens/Alternative Party (Table 4) and Social Democratic Party (Table 5) place themselves to all five major parties on a left-right continuum. What we saw in Chart 2 is more precisely analyzed in Table 4: Green supporters distance themselves from all the established parties, but they are much closer to the SPD than to the other three. As for those who identify with the SPD, Table 5 shows that they place themselves closer to the Greens/Alternatives than to any other party on the left-right continuum, excepting of course the SPD itself.

TABLE 4
How Close Green/Alternative Supporters Place Themselves to the Parties on a Left-Right Continuum

| Greens | SPD | FDP | CDU | CSU |
|---|---|---|---|---|
| 0.9 | 1.4 | 4.2 | 5.6 | 6.6 |

### TABLE 5
### How Close SPD Supporters Place Themselves to the Parties on a Left-Right Continuum

| SPD | Greens | FDP | CDU | CSU |
|---|---|---|---|---|
| 0.8 | 2.1 | 2.3 | 3.5 | 4.7 |

At the same time, Social Democratic supporters do not distance themselves too greatly from the Free Democratic Party, which demonstrates the broad range of perspectives among the SPD identifiers: the left wing feels close to the Greens and the more moderate wing closer to the Free Democrats. But both Tables 4 and 5 demonstrate the relatively small gap between Greens/Alternatives and SPD identifiers. The same can be shown by analyzing the "sympathy ranking" of the different parties by those who identify with the SPD and Greens/Alternatives respectively:

### TABLE 6
### Sympathy Ranking of the German Parties by Green/Alternative and SPD Identifiers

|  | SPD | Greens | FDP | CDU/CSU |
|---|---|---|---|---|
| SPD Party Identifiers | 9.7 | 6.5 | 5.1 | 4.7 |
| Green/Alternative Party Identifiers | 2.6 | 8.2 | 2.1 | 1.3 |

These figures also show that the Green identifiers have very little sympathy for the other parties, although the SPD ranks a little higher than the others. This underlines the characterization of the Greens/Alternatives as a fundamental opposition party.

### The Future of the Greens/Alternatives

The question remains as to the likely evolution of the Green/Alternative movement and the West German party system. Since the loss of governing power in Bonn, the SPD has been trying to reintegrate the Green/Alternative movement. On the night of the state election in Hesse on September 26, 1982, Willy Brandt began talking about the necessity of building a new coalition of voters consisting of socialists, social democrats, the peace movement, and the women's movement. In the federal election campaign of 1983 the SPD's candidate for the office of the chancellor, Hans Jochen Vogel, tried to demonstrate his openmindedness toward the Green/Alternative movement with regard to their demands—although he did this cautiously enough so as not to diminish his support among

SPD voters of the political center. Since the election of March 6, the SPD has been attempting more intensively to reintegrate the Green/Alternative movement, and one can safely forecast that it will make even greater efforts to do so by adopting at least some of the movement's positions. Thus, one can expect the SPD increasingly to oppose the NATO dual-track INF modernization decision. Also, it seems probable that the SPD will seek to co-opt the Green/Alternative opposition to any kind of nuclear energy, and to adopt some of its positions with regard to economic and social policy as well.

The SPD has already been partly successful in wooing the Greens/Alternatives to its ranks. At the time the CDU/CSU-FDP coalition was formed in October 1982, the Green/Alternative support was estimated at about 8 percent of the electorate. It comprised only 5.6 percent on March 6, 1983. Only one week later, Schleswig-Holstein's SPD, which is perceived as being a party of the left wing, managed to push the local Greens back beneath the 5 percent threshold. The Greens also failed to get 5 percent in the state election in Rhineland-Palatinate, which was held on March 6, but this may be less significant because the social structure of this state is less favorable to the Greens/Alternatives.

The most likely scenario for the future looks like this: The SPD will continue its attempts to integrate Green/Alternative movement voters, and to do this it will take over leftist positions on an increasing scale. To the extent that it will be successful, the SPD will push the Greens/Alternatives out of the federal Parliament. Such a development, however, explains one of the dilemmas of the SPD, which was formulated by Richard Löwenthal in a controversy with Willy Brandt in the SPD's Journal, *Neue Gesellschaft (New Society)*, in November 1981. The more successful the SPD is in attracting the Greens/Alternatives, the more voters from the political center the party will lose. Moreover, a SPD which succeeds in integrating the Greens/Alternatives will lose the federal election of 1987 because it will no longer be supported by substantial numbers of voters from the political center. By that time, however, the SPD's leadership structure will be a different one: the leading personalities of the SPD's days as the governing party during the tenure of Chancellor Schmidt will no longer play an important role. By then, the SPD leadership will be oriented to the left, will fail to draw the proper consequences from the defeat in the election of 1987, and will continue increasingly to espouse positions of the political Left. If so, it will then lose the federal election of 1991.

By the early 1990s, however, it will have integrated the Green/Alternative movement firmly enough so that the party may rise against the series of electoral defeats, look toward a new orientation, and increasingly seek the support of voters from the political center, just as was the case at the end of the 1950s with the Godesberger Program. On this basis the party will be able to stabilize itself by 1995 and will again compete seriously for political power in Bonn by 1999. Perhaps with this scenario in mind, the grand old strategist of the SPD, Herbert Wehner, who had led the party into the Grand Coalition and to leadership of the government, predicted after the loss of governing power in the fall of 1982 that the SPD would have to face about 15 years in opposition.

This scenario, of course, would probably come apart in the event the other side makes major political mistakes. Here one only has to recall that, after President Nixon's great success in the election of 1972, many in the United States saw an enduring Republican majority, in favor of which there were indeed plausible arguments at that time. However, no one then could predict the impact of Watergate which contributed to the election in 1976 of Jimmy Carter. Such events are unforeseeable, with obvious implications for the scenario outlined above. What is important, however, is not the stated assumption about the duration of the SPD's period in opposition, but the prediction of the rise and fall of the Greens/Alternatives, on the one hand, and the development of the SPD, on the other, set forth in this scenario. If the SPD regains governing power in 1999 and keeps it for a considerable period of time, the next Green/Alternative movement could be expected to begin to form about the year 2012. Whatever the concrete occasion might be, the reason for the emergence of a new protest movement could again be traced to the fact that in a dichotomized party system the party of change would have been in power too long.

### Implications for German Politics

What does the foregoing analysis mean for the future of German politics? The presence of the Greens in Parliament will make it more difficult to conduct legislative meetings according to the rules of procedure. Of greater significance is the fact that because the outcome of the election of March 6, 1983, was a clear majority for the government of the CDU/CSU and FDP, the Greens' entry into Parliament will have only limited influence on the substantive policy of the Federal Republic. This stands in contrast to the nightmare that overshadowed West German politics in the winter of 1982/83 when quite a few people feared that the CDU/CSU might fail to win a majority and that the FDP would not be returned to parliament, and therefore that the Greens/Alternatives would play a crucial role in the formation of a SPD minority government—as in Hamburg between June and December 1982 and in Hesse since September 1982. The experience in both state parliaments shows that, even if the SPD tries to compromise as much as possible with these groups, they are structurally unable to deliver reliable support for any kind of government. Therefore, in Hamburg and Hesse early elections were called. In Hamburg this led to a clear SPD victory. In Hesse an election was scheduled for September 24, 1983. It is entirely likely that yet another early *federal* election would have been held if the aforementioned nightmare had become reality in March 1983.

What is more important now is the fact that the Greens/Alternatives in Parliament will provide an institutionalized temptation for the SPD to take over their symbolic positions, a consequence of which will be that the basic principles of German domestic and foreign policy will no longer be sustained by the bipartisan consensus that obtained in the 1960s and 1970s. In this context, one should remember that in the 1950s Konrad Adenauer and Ludwig Erhard built the Federal Republic on two pillars: namely, the organization of a free society in an economic system of market economy, and the integration of the Federal Republic into the Western alliance system. As the party of the opposition, the SPD had strongly opposed both decisions and had achieved participation in, and later leadership of, the government only when it accepted both principles. With the Godesberger Program of 1959 it accepted a market economy, and with Herbert Wehner's famous speech in June 1960 in the German Parliament, the SPD accepted the integration of the Federal Republic into the Western alliance as the basis of Social Democratic foreign policy.

With this transformation of the SPD, Chancellor Brandt, Minister of Economics Schiller, Minister of Finance Schmidt, and later Chancellor Schmidt became guarantors of the Federal Republic of Germany as a loyal member of the Atlantic Alliance, as well as a supporter of the principles of a market economy. It is noteworthy that the SPD lost governing power when it assumed at least ambiguous positions on these two issues. At its party convention in Munich in April 1982, after long debates in which Chancellor Schmidt—who considered himself to have a superior competence with regard to economics—did not take part, the SPD took decisions that were in no way compatible with a market-economy system. At the same time, this party convention made it clear that the SPD would not be able to muster a majority for the NATO dual-track decision which had been initiated by SPD Chancellor Schmidt in 1977.

Inevitably, the basic principles of German domestic and foreign policy will be debated on an increasing scale in the next decade between government and opposition, a situation that had occurred once before in the 1950s. Other nations will no doubt be increasingly interested in the outcome of elections in West Germany—as was already manifested during the campaign leading to the federal election of March 1983, when a strange international coalition, including French and Italian Socialists, Conservatives from Britain and Norway, and Republicans and Democrats in the United States, hoped for Helmut Kohl's success, while the Soviet Union desired that Hans Jochen Vogel would be the winner.

With regard to short-term consequences, one can expect that the Helmut Kohl Government will support deployment of new intermediate-range missiles in accordance with the NATO decision of December 1979. This will surely result in widespread protest demonstrations and even the use of violence on the part of Green/Alternative followers in cooperation with the "peace movement." Television networks in Western countries will then show film clips that will seem to indicate an intensification of civil strife in West Germany. Viewers, however, should not forget that even if 200,000 demonstrators should take part in such activities, this would be about the same number who attend soccer games each weekend in the Federal Republic. Compared to an electorate of 40,000,000 people, these demonstrations represent an activity involving a very small minority.

One should also be aware that this protest is only superficially directed against the deployment of new missiles, just as the protest in 1982 against the construction of a new runway at the Frankfurt Airport and actions against nuclear energy were only temporary manifestations of a more profound protest. It is characteristic of the Greens/Alternatives, in the final analysis, that they question the basic principles of representative government, according to which a government that has won a majority in parliament in free elections has the right and the duty to decide and to implement its policies. A minority of the Greens/Alternatives asserts its "democratic" right to oppose such decisions for moral or other reasons. At the same time, they question the authority of the democratic process with regard to those issues considered to be central to its vitality as a political system. They claim the right to decide which issues are to be resolved by the normal processes of constitutional government and which issues shall be decided by the veto of a minority group.

This basic attitude corresponds more to the Leninist principle of the party as the vanguard of the proletariat, where a minority is alleged to know what is best for the majority, than it does to the tenets of parliamentary democracy and political pluralism of societies on both sides of the Atlantic. The approach advocated by the Greens is not compatible with the principles of representative government. Viewed from this perspective, the Green/Alternative movement is much more than the organization of protest against environmental damage and more than the articulation of the frustrations of the restive elements of German society. It is no less than the questioning of basic principles of representative government. This posture, of course, has been developed and is understood only by the Greens' hard core, the inner circle described earlier. It is, to a large degree, the result of a long, confusing and inconclusive discussion on how to "democratize" German society that took place in the late 1960s and early 1970s.

## Conclusion

To understand the Greens/Alternatives, it is important to differentiate between the activists and the supporters as a whole. The supporters will soon be reintegrated into the party system: While the Greens/Alternatives were once able to attract those Social Democrats who became disenchanted with the Schmidt Government's centrist policies, the SPD leadership in opposition has moved leftward and already has begun to regain much of that lost support. The activist core of the Greens, of course, will not be reintegrated. Because some leading members of the Greens originally came from the SPD, it cannot be ruled out that, especially from the younger ranks, some will eventually rejoin the Social Democrats. Of the two segments of the Green/Alternative hard core, the "true believers" will most likely resign when they realize that they no longer can attract public support. The communists, after realizing that they have failed under the Green flag, will develop other tactics of subversion.

# INSTITUTE FOR FOREIGN POLICY ANALYSIS, INC.
## List of Publications

### Special Reports

THE CRUISE MISSILE: BARGAINING CHIP OR DEFENSE BARGAIN? By Robert L. Pfaltzgraff, Jr., and Jacquelyn K. Davis. January 1977. x, 53pp. $3.00.

EUROCOMMUNISM AND THE ATLANTIC ALLIANCE. By James E. Dougherty and Diane K. Pfaltzgraff. January 1977. xiv, 66pp. $3.00.

THE NEUTRON BOMB: POLITICAL, TECHNICAL AND MILITARY ISSUES. By S. T. Cohen. November 1978. xii, 95pp. $6.50.

SALT II AND U.S.-SOVIET STRATEGIC FORCES. By Jacquelyn K. Davis, Patrick J. Friel and Robert L. Pfaltzgraff, Jr. June 1979. xii, 51pp. $5.00.

THE EMERGING STRATEGIC ENVIRONMENT: IMPLICATIONS FOR BALLISTIC MISSILE DEFENSE. By Leon Gouré, William G. Hyland and Colin S. Gray. December 1979. xi, 75pp. $6.50.

THE SOVIET UNION AND BALLISTIC MISSILE DEFENSE. By Jacquelyn K. Davis, Uri Ra'anan, Robert L. Pfaltzgraff, Jr., Michael J. Deane and John M. Collins. March 1980. xi, 71pp. $6.50 (Out of print.)

ENERGY ISSUES AND ALLIANCE RELATIONSHIPS: THE UNITED STATES, WESTERN EUROPE AND JAPAN. By Robert L. Pfaltzgraff, Jr. April 1980. xii, 71pp. $6.50.

U.S. STRATEGIC-NUCLEAR POLICY AND BALLISTIC MISSILE DEFENSE: THE 1980S AND BEYOND. By William Schneider, Jr., Donald G. Brennan, William A. Davis, Jr., and Hans Rühle. April 1980. xii, 61pp. $6.50.

THE UNNOTICED CHALLENGE: SOVIET MARITIME STRATEGY AND THE GLOBAL CHOKE POINTS. By Robert J. Hanks, August 1980. xi, 66pp. $6.50.

FORCE REDUCTIONS IN EUROPE: STARTING OVER. By Jeffrey Record. October 1980. xi, 92pp. $6.50.

SALT II AND AMERICAN SECURITY. By Gordon J. Humphrey, William R. Van Cleave, Jeffrey Record, William H. Kincade, and Richard Perle. October 1980. xvi, 65pp.

THE FUTURE OF U.S. LAND-BASED STRATEGIC FORCES. By Jake Garn, J.I. Coffey, Lord Chalfont, and Ellery B. Block. December 1980. xvi, 80 pp.

THE CAPE ROUTE: IMPERILED WESTERN LIFELINE. By Robert J. Hanks. February 1981. xi, 80pp. $6.50 (Hardcover, $10.00).

THE RAPID DEPLOYMENT FORCE AND U.S. MILITARY INTERVENTION IN THE PERSIAN GULF. By Jeffrey Record. February 1981. viii, 82pp. $7.50 (Hardcover, $12.00).

POWER PROJECTION AND THE LONG-RANGE COMBAT AIRCRAFT: MISSIONS, CAPABILITIES, AND ALTERNATIVE DESIGNS. By Jacquelyn K. Davis and Robert L. Pfaltzgraff, Jr. June 1981. ix, 37pp. $6.50.

THE PACIFIC FAR EAST: ENDANGERED AMERICAN STRATEGIC POSITION. By Robert J. Hanks. October 1981. ix, 75pp. $7.50.

NATO'S THEATER NUCLEAR FORCE MODERNIZATION PROGRAM: THE REAL ISSUES. By Jeffrey Record. November 1981. vii, 102pp. $7.50.

THE CHEMISTRY OF DEFEAT: ASYMMETRIES IN U.S. AND SOVIET CHEMICAL WARFARE POSTURES. By Amoretta M. Hoeber, December 1981. xiii, 91pp. $6.50.

*The Horn of Africa: A Map of Political-Strategic Conflict.* By James E. Dougherty. April 1982. xv, 74pp. $7.50.

*The West, Japan and Cape Route Imports: The Oil and Non-Fuel Mineral Trades.* By Charles Perry. June 1982. xiv, 88pp. $7.50.

## Foreign Policy Reports

The papers in this series of Foreign Policy Reports are addressed to a variety of topics in the field of world affairs, including diplomacy, economics, strategy, science and technology, arms control, international organization, and country and regional issues.

*Defense Technology and the Atlantic Alliance: Competition or Collaboration?* By Frank T. J. Bray and Michael Moodie. April 1977. 42pp. $5.00.

*Iran's Quest for Security: U.S. Arms Transfers and the Nuclear Option.* By Alvin J. Cottrell and James E. Dougherty. May 1977. 59pp. $5.00.

*Ethiopia, the Horn of Africa, and U.S. Policy.* By John H. Spencer. September 1977. 69pp. $5.00 (Out of print.)

*Beyond the Arab-Israeli Settlement: New Directions for U.S. Policy in the Middle East.* By R. K. Ramazani. September 1977. 69pp. $5.00.

*Spain, the Monarchy and the Atlantic Community.* By David C. Jordan. June 1979. 55pp. $5.00.

*U.S. Strategy at the Crossroads: Two Views.* By Robert J. Hanks and Jeffrey Record. July 1982. 69pp. $7.50.

*The U.S. Military Presence in the Middle East: Problems and Prospects.* By Robert J. Hanks. December 1982. vii, 77pp. $7.50.

*Southern Africa and Western Security.* By Robert J. Hanks. August 1983. vii, 71pp. $7.50.

## Books

*Atlantic Community in Crisis: A Redefinition of the Atlantic Relationship.* Edited by Walter F. Hahn and Robert L. Pfaltzgraff, Jr. Pergamon Press, 1979. 386pp. $43.00.

*Soviet Military Strategy in Europe.* By Joseph D. Douglass, Jr. Pergamon Press, 1980. 252pp. $33.00.

*The Warsaw Pact: Arms, Doctrine and Strategy.* By William J. Lewis. 1982. 471pp. $19.95.

## Conference Reports

*NATO and Its Future: A German-American Roundtable.* Summary of a Dialogue. 1978. 22pp. $1.00.

*Second German-American Roundtable on NATO: The Theater Nuclear Balance.* A Conference Report. 1978. 32pp. $1.00.

*The Soviet Union and Ballistic Missile Defense.* A Conference Report. 1978. 26pp. $1.00.

*U.S. Strategic-Nuclear Policy and Ballistic Missile Defense: The 1980s and Beyond.* A Conference Report. 1979. 30 pp. $1.00.

*SALT II and American Security.* A Conference Report. 1979. 39pp.

*The Future of U.S. Land-Based Strategic Forces.* A Conference Report. 1979. 32pp.

THE FUTURE OF NUCLEAR POWER. A Conference Report. 1980. 48pp. $1.00.

THIRD GERMAN-AMERICAN ROUNDTABLE ON NATO: MUTUAL AND BALANCED FORCE REDUCTIONS IN EUROPE. A Conference Report. 1980. 27pp. $1.00.

FOURTH GERMAN-AMERICAN ROUNDTABLE ON NATO: NATO MODERNIZATION AND EUROPEAN SECURITY. A Conference Report. 1981. 15pp. $1.00.

SECOND ANGLO-AMERICAN SYMPOSIUM ON DETERRENCE AND EUROPEAN SECURITY. A Conference Report. 1981. 25pp. $1.00.

THE U.S. DEFENSE MOBILIZATION INFRASTRUCTURE: PROBLEMS AND PRIORITIES. A Conference Report (A Conference sponsored by the International Security Studies Program, The Fletcher School of Law and Diplomacy, Tufts University). 1981. 25pp. $1.00.

U.S. STRATEGIC DOCTRINE FOR THE 1980S. A Conference Report. 1982. 14 pp.

FRENCH-AMERICAN SYMPOSIUM ON STRATEGY, DETERRENCE AND EUROPEAN SECURITY. A Conference Report. 1982. 14 pp. $1.00.

FIFTH GERMAN-AMERICAN ROUNDTABLE ON NATO: THE CHANGING CONTEXT OF THE EUROPEAN SECURITY DEBATE. Summary of a Transatlantic Dialogue. A Conference Report. 1982. 22pp. $1.00.

ENERGY SECURITY AND THE FUTURE OF NUCLEAR POWER. A Conference Report. 1982. 39pp. $2.50.

INTERNATIONAL SECURITY DIMENSIONS OF SPACE. A Conference Report (The Eleventh Annual Conference, sponsored by the International Security Studies Program, The Fletcher School of Law and Diplomacy, Tufts University). 1982. 24pp. $2.50.

PORTUGAL, SPAIN AND TRANSATLANTIC RELATIONS. Summary of a Transatlantic Dialogue. A Conference Report. 1983. 18pp. $2.50.

JAPANESE-AMERICAN SYMPOSIUM ON REDUCING STRATEGIC MINERALS VULNERABILITIES: CURRENT PLANS, PRIORITIES AND POSSIBILITIES FOR COOPERATION. A Conference Report. 1983. 31pp. $2.50.

NATIONAL SECURITY POLICY: THE DECISION-MAKING PROCESS. A Conference Report (The Twelfth Annual Conference, sponsored by the International Security Studies Program, The Fletcher School of Law and Diplomacy, Tufts University). 1983. 28pp. $2.50.